Rogue Sa

by

Task-Force-Sheepdog
- operation-education -

from the
Maine Republic Email Alert
3 Linnell Circle
Brunswick, Maine 04011

www.mainerepublicemailalert.com

ROGUE-SABRE-1

CONTENTS

ROGUE-SABRE-1

December 12, 2016

The following Report and Intelligence Briefing is brought to you by a former, US Armed Forces Special Operations Soldier and an elite member of the Psychological Operations (Warfare) Regiment of the US Army's Special Operations Forces Community. His military experience resides with the United States Special Operations Command (USSOCOM), United States Army Civil Affairs and Psychological Operations Command (USACAPOC), and Special Operations Forces (SOF) during the years of 1999-2012.

This gentleman patriot is known as **ROGUE-SABRE-1**, others may know him as **SERGEANT BILLY**. Today he has authorized a public release of his "final" report to the people of the world, and especially for the attention of the US Special Operations Forces and the Militia [people] of The United States of America. The 84-page briefing and subject matter adapted to this book can be described as an **"Operational attempt to stop the Illegal takeover and surrender of the 50 Sovereign Nation States of North America, known as The United States of America."**

ROGUE-SABRE-1 has allowed the Ascension With Earth blog to present his message to the world, and in doing so, they have uploaded his intelligence briefing to his Scribd account for people to view, download, and share.

Many readers of this blog will be familiar with the subject matter at hand and will be able to get a deeper understanding of the USA history of the republic and the USA Corporation, through the eyes of a patriotic military soldier.

You can view the report at the following link....
https://www.scribd.com/document/334045920/ROGUE-SABRE-1-An-OP-ED-By-Former-US-Armed-Forces-Special-Operations-Soldier

TASK-FORCE-SHEEPDOG
- (OPERATION-EDUCATION) -

11 NOV 2016

:ID#~00212X

UNCLASSIFIED

FOR THE ATTENTION OF: US Special Operations Forces and the Militia [people] of The United-States of America.

SUBJECT: The Operational Attempt to stop the Illegal takeover and surrender of the 50 Sovereign Nation States of North America, known as The United States of America.

REPORT OBJECTIVE:

~A. EXPLAIN, and demonstrate to both members of the US Military and the People of the United States, that there is an attempt to SECRETLY and ILLEGALLY TAKEOVER and QUIETLY-SURRENDER, The United States of America back over into the hands, of the British Crown.

~B. PROVE, beyond any shadow of a doubt, to the Members of the US Military and to the People of the United States, that the attempt to takeover and surrender this Nation to the British Crown is illegal and an act of absolute fraud. And in so-doing, show them that their prayers to GOD to save this Nation, have been answered.

OVERALL OUTLINE: The individuals, and activities of the entities that will be identified and discussed, within this report are:

~C. **The Royal Family Members** at the very top of world control, i.e. **"The Tribe of DAN"**, who are the framers and architects of

"THE EMPIRE OF THE 3 CITY STATES", consisting of, **London City, the District of Columbia's City-State, and the City-State of the Vatican**, and their Melita, "the JESUITS"; this conglomeration more well known as, **"The New World Order"** (N.W.O.) ; – The 3 "Unclean Spirits" identified in the Book of Revelations; **GREED**= [London City] / **POWER**= [City-State of the District of Columbia] / **CONTROL**= [City-State of the Vatican] -

~D. And **the American Warriors at the very tip of the spear**, who stand in opposition of, "The Tribe of DAN" :**FEDERAL-POSTAL-JUDGE, POSTMASTER-GENERAL, COMMANDER-AND-CHIEF, :Russell-Jay:Gould** and his accomplice, witness, and Global Corporate Government Partner, :**FEDERAL-POSTAL-JUDGE, :David-Wynn: Miller.** -- Self Appointed, **American Common Law Judge :Anna-Von: Reitz.** – **and members of the 11 TH and 7TH SPECIAL OPERATIONS GROUP(S) USSOCOM/ USACAPOC/SOF.**

~0. For my name is :**[name redacted]**. I am a 9th Generation American & :American-War-Fighter. As a Patriot, and descendant of whom both Great-Grand-Fathers on both sides of my family-tree, fought along-side and under the Military Command of General George Washington during the American Revolutionary War - I can assure you - that I have been ever vigilant in my watch over this nation as my family's heir to this great responsibility.

~1. For I am a Former, US Armed Forces Special Operations Soldier and an elite member of the Psychological Operations (Warfare) Regiment of the US Army's Special Operations Forces Community. – USSOCOM/USACAPOC/SOF (1999-2012)

PSYOP CAPABILITY (CAPES) BRIEF:
a.) Psychological Operations (Warfare) is the tip of the spear and the highest echelon of Military Warfare in the world who's mission objectives are to conduct – amongst many other things - Planned Operations to Convey Selected Information and Indicators to a specific demographic or target audience in order to:

b.) Infiltrate to Change, Persuade and/or Influence the Emotions, Motives, Objective Reasoning and <u>Ultimately the Personal Behavior</u> of any Target Audience(s), Foreign or otherwise - on a planetary scale if need be - in an effort to control every Town, City, State, Government, Organization(s), Group(s), or Individual(s); from their Religious Groups to their Corporations all the way down to their Clubs and/or their Teams, in an entire Country/Nation or Region of the Hemisphere of this planet, in association and in cooperation with the US State Department, Host Nation, and Commander in Chief's (CINC) Overall Objectives.

~2. For this is my Official Military Report and a Personal Account of what I have come to know and understand as - not just the truth - but the facts that are being withheld from the Military and the American People of this great Nation. FACT'S, that will NULLIFY EVERY LAW and every last Tyrannical piece of LEGISLATION that has been illegally introduced and rammed down the throat of this nation since 1999, THEREBY SETTING THE ENTIRE COUNTRY FREE, AND ENDING THE ORCHESTRATED DEGRADATION of the United States of America, once and for all.

The United States of America is NO LONGER under the Command and/or Control, or the oversight of the current "Administration" posing as the Leadership in Washington DC. Neither does this Country have a "President", a "Congress", nor a Senate... and the entire Legislative and Judicial System, to include all Civil Authority, has been suspended and Officially, Legally and Lawfully shut down and closed, since 2 NOV 1999.

This Country has, since 2 NOV 1999 to current date, been in a state of MARTIAL LAW.

----- AND YOU NEED TO KNOW, HOW AND WHY -----

PRELUDE

FACT: 2 NOV 1999, due to THE RULES OF INTERNATIONAL BANKING LAW, the "Bank- Note", aka The U.S. Constitution - which was a Postal-Command-Contract-Location-Accord - [a Postmaster General contract agreement (Treaty) making the king, the Postmaster General for the 13 colonies, allowing him to capture, control and bilk them through commerce] struck between the king of GB and the Founders of the Republic of the united States – which had officially come to an end 2 NOV 1999, and with that, all Federal Services Contracts between the King of Great Britain and the 13 Colonies, (now 50 States of the Union of the Republic) known as **"the united States of America"** were - and have been since 2 NOV 1999 - Legally and Lawfully, dissolved and Ended. –

The kings Contract Agencies were Legally and Lawfully dissolved, along with their standing and their jurisdiction as the Federal Enforcement of the king of Great Britain and his laws on 2 NOV 1999, when his Contract as Postmaster General (capture of the Colonies in commerce) for the now 50 States, Legally and Lawfully came to an international end, thereby closing his Post Office in DC down. When he VACATED (which he only had to do temporarily) he was LEGALLY and LAWFULLY back-doored and replaced as our international representative in commerce, by a new POSTMASTER-GENERAL in a HEROIC EFFORT to STOP the TYRANNY and END the FRAUD against this Nation,… if not the World itself. – Tyranny and FRAUD that everyone WONT STOP CRYING ABOUT and won't SHUT- UP for long enough about to ACTUALLY RESEARCH, RECOGNIZE and REALIZE what the hell just happened in this Nation that the king of GB, the IMF, and the Vatican are very well aware of.

That means that all of the Laws, and/or the "Codes and Statutes of Public Justice", and the entities that enforce them, ATF, FBI, NSA,

12

that have all been created by the king of GB to enforce the rule of his laws here in this country, IRS, DEA, DHS, ARE GONE!

As these legally defunct entities are now lawfully dissolved, they therefore possess no Authorization to execute Operations, nor execute any Operations to enforce that now nullified former Federal British Authority anywhere within the Continental United States of America. As the Agency Authorizations for the British run Federal Government Services Corporation are no longer Lawfully Valid, they then have no Legal Standing to operate in the capacity of legal or lawful extensions of that now DEFUNCT Private Corporate Contracted British Run Government Entity.

A Private, British Federal Contract Government Services Corporation,…(aka the Presidential "Administration") that illegally continues - void of a Legal National Federal Contract - to fraudulently enforce the provision of these DEFUNCT Federal Services upon both the States, and the people of this Nation. An illegal British Federal Government Services Corporation, that continues to illegally operate, in and out of the PRIVATE, CORPORATE Municipal City State of the District of Columbia. Which itself is a Private Foreign Enclave that was, in effect, built to host a PRIVATE- FEDERAL-POSTAL-CONTRACT-VENUE FOR THE CONTROL OF COMMERCE that they NO LONGER HAVE LEGAL or LAWFUL JURISDICTION TO EXIST IN, and their TACTICAL CONTROL in this CAPACITY has been LIQUIDATED.

The FACT is, they have NO LEGAL or LAWFUL POWER to enforce those now TERMINATED Private Corporate Federal Government Contract Services "Codes & Statutes of Public Justice" (Laws, Mandates and/or Executive Orders of any kind) anywhere here in the United States… and therefore as absolutely none of it is Legal or Lawful, they are nothing more than extensions of a LEGALLY DEFUNCT Private Government Services Corporation and rogue foreign entities, operating illegally on our shores – working inland - in an act of Piracy and Fraud by IMPERSONATING actual Government sponsored Agencies of the United States of America. And this once Contracted Federal Government Services Corporation, is doing all of this with the purposeful intent to wreak and insight civil havoc in acts of Terrorism against all they encounter in a continued effort to extort money and property from them. THIS IS GREAT BRITAIN, REFUSING TO STEP DOWN and RELINQUISH THEIR POSTAL-COMMAND and CONTROL TO THE NEW POSTMAS-TER-GENERAL,... AND THIS IS BECAUSE THEY DO NOT WANT TO ADMIT THAT THEY WERE BEATEN ACROSS THE BOARD BY THE NEW POSTMASTER-GENERAL,... THEREBY HAVING THEIR TAILS HANDED TO THEM BY HIM,... AND LOST EVERYTHING ELSE AS WELL ALONG WITH IT IN THE PROCESS,... that NO ONE but them, is even cognizant of, And they want it to stay that way.

Time to wake up.

How? – And what does that mean? – ... It means that, in 1999, all of the Federal Agencies in the United States, from the Post Office, to the President, to Congress, to the Senate, and the Supreme Court, all the way on down, were Legally and Lawfully dissolved and ended when they were replaced by a new POSTMASTER-GENERAL. But they refuse to relinquish Command and Control over to the new POSTMASTER-GENERAL who, with National Recognition for who he is and what he's done,... AS HE IS AN AMERICAN,... Will end their Tyranny and their illegal Rule over us,. FOREVER.

~3. For in order that this report make sense, history as we have been taught and therefore made to understand, must be revisited in brief manners and retaught throughout this report as we move forward in order to bring the reader full circle, with a greater understanding of and for, passed national events.

GLOBAL WARFARE - 101

~4. The most important thing that you need to know and understand is the fact that on 22 OCT 1871 this entire planet and everyone on it, was "captured" in a "shipping war", (shipping wars) where everyone and everything in this shipping war has been placed and is/are, under the International Jurisdiction of Admiralty and Maritime Law of the Sea, in a global warfare effort to control all COMMERCE on Planet Earth.

This is what the YELLOW FRINGE AROUND THE FLAG SIGNI-FIES. It is INDICATING that it has been CAPTURED by a PRI-VATE CORPORATION in a Shipping War under the jurisdiction of Admiralty and Maritime Law of the Sea, identified as advertised by the YELLOW ROPE-FRINGE ENCIRCLING IT. (Capturing it). It is broadcasting and advertising that since it has been captured, we have been infiltrated, taken control of and captured as well, and are therefore in a State of Martial Law. Wherein, when beaten-down and dragged into a Court, are guilty until PROVEN innocent, where we are charged with crimes and extorted by punishments that are foreign to our civil systems, and our soil.

Anywhere that the U.S. Flag is located with a YELLOW FRINGE AROUND IT, it is advertising that in those VENUES, or at that/ those Corporate-Contract-Location(s), the Laws of Admiralty super-sede our Nations Declarative Standing associated with the Law of our Flag that flies in opposition to those Laws, as properly repre-sented by our Nations Flag WITHOUT the Yellow Fringe around it. Yet as it is CAPTURED by that fringe, it is therefore "BOUND" [Contracted] to authorize those locations to harvest our country in whatever way stipulated. These are usually at your Court-Houses and County Recorder or State Buildings; the locations where you would pay your FINES $$ and FEES $$ at.

LAW OF THE FLAG

The United States Flag Code outlines certain guidelines for the use, display, and disposal of the flag. For example, the flag should never be dipped to any person or thing, unless it is the ensign responding to a salute from a ship of a foreign nation. This tradition comes from the 1908 Summer Olympics in London, where countries were asked to dip their flag to King Edward VII: **the American flag bearer did not.**

15

<u>Team captain Martin Sheridan</u> is famously quoted as saying, - **"This flag dips to no earthly king!"**.

Sppecifications : U.S.C. Title; 4 – 1X1.9 Dimensional, "G-spec" government specification, federal flag.

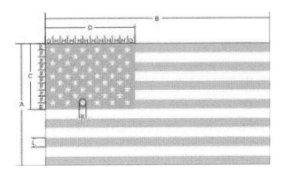

The basic design of the current flag is specified by 4 U.S.C. [§ 1; 4 U.S.C. § 2 outlines the addition of new stars to represent new states. The specification gives the following values:

•Hoist (height) of the flag: A = 1.0
•Fly (width) of the flag: B = 1.9
•Hoist (height) of the canton ("union"): C = 0.5385 (A × 7/13, spanning seven stripes)
•Fly (width) of the canton: D = 0.76 (B × 2/5, two-fifths of the flag width)
•E = F = 0.0538 (C/10, One-tenth of the height of the canton)
•G = H = 0.0633 (D/12, One twelfth of the width of the canton)
•Diameter of star: K = 0.0616 (L × 4/5, four-fifths of the stripe width, the calculation only gives 0.0616 if L is first rounded to 0.077)
•Width of stripe: L = 0.0769 (A/13, One thirteenth of the flag height)

•These specifications are contained in an executive order which, strictly speaking, governs only flags made for or by the U.S. federal government. In practice, most U.S. national flags available for sale to the public have a different width-to-height ratio; common sizes are 2 × 3 ft. or 4 × 6 ft. (flag ratio 1.5), 2.5 × 4 ft. or 5 × 8 ft. (1.6), or 3 × 5 ft. or 6 × 10 ft. (1.667). Even flags flown over the U.S. Capitol for sale to the public through Representatives or Senators are provided in these sizes. **Flags that are made to the prescribed 1.9 ratio are often referred to as "G-spec" (for "government specification") flags.**

ANYTHING that stands above the flag itself, in its position attached to the top of the flag-pole, suspends the contract or, the Standing of the flag itself, and therefore, lets you know what, or whose venue that you are in; Vatican Banking, Presidential Venue, etc.. In other words, at that location where your flag flies, the laws of your flag no longer apply at that Corporate Contract Location, as its National Standing – to include yours – has been subdued and/or disqualified and suspended by whatever is attached to the TOP of the Flag-Pole. Those positions are classified as DOMESTIC ENEMIES to the Government of the People of the United States Territories; i.e. California, Nevada, etc... and are to be considered legally and lawfully closed, since 2 NOV 1999.

A SPIRE on the flag-pole (anywhere you see it) lets you know that you are in a military court-martial venue and is declaring a state of war [Martial-Law] against the people. Every State Governors Office in The United States has a SPIRE on the flag pole, denoting that they are at war with their people; and have been since 2 NOV 1999.

An Eagle (Wing tips are up) on the flag-pole, means that you are in a PRESIDENTIAL Venue.

A Phoenix (Wing tips pointed down) denotes that you are in a VATICAN Banking Venue. In your County Offices, where you would pay your fines, or purchase a copy of your Deed of Trust, you will see a Phoenix on the top of the flag-pole, which tells you that you are paying your money to the VATICAN and/or its banking system.

A Ball on top of the flag-pole, denotes that it is recruiting contract(s) at that location.

The original flag of our country NEVER had a Yellow-Fringe around it. A Yellow-Fringe denotes that you are under the international Jurisdiction of Admiralty and Maritime Law of the Sea. It also denotes that this flag is a Private "Corporate" Flag, as it is flown by the Federal Corporation in the District of Columbia; it's a Corporate flag. Corporations are operating under the international jurisdiction of the sea and therefore the Maxims of Ecclesiastical Law, aka, "Corporate" Federal, [Roman] Law; i.e. DESPOTIC MAN MADE LAWS OF THE VATICAN.

~5. For a fact, the IRS claims that they work for the United States Treasury. The United States Treasury is under the jurisdiction of the United States Post Office. The Post Office is responsible for all 3,850 branches of Government. Because the Post Office, when established on 22 OCT 1871, in an act of global warfare, Captured the entire world and all "Vessels" in it, in an effort to command and control all Commerce of Planet Earth. [Contracts, people, money, cars, etc..]

The International Jurisdiction of Admiralty and Maritime Law of the Sea is/are the Law(s) of the king of Great Britain, wherein everyone and everything is recognized as a little boat, or VESSEL that is floating around in a "Sea of Space", as "Vessel's", and are therefore, and have been, captured in the kings Global Feudal System of COMMERCE; i.e. the shipping [movement] of everyone and everything on the Planet... and the "Time-lines" [shipping-date-movements] working in conjunction with the entire operation were set up and are controlled by the Vatican's "Gregorian Calender" and the Global Position of the Post-Office of the Universal Postmaster General up in BERN Switzerland. Where all of the Post Offices of the kings and/or monarchs and dictators of the world are registered and their Wars are conducted though. POSTAL WARS. SHIPPING WARS. COMMERCE. The control of the shipping and movement of all cargoes and/or vessels, i.e. people, money, boats, planes, cars, military, and/or,... yes,... WARS on Planet Earth. All in an effort to state the claim that they own [have captured] everything, and the planet, to include you.

Under Maritime Law, TITLE: 46,-~Ch.,-~1.,-~Sec.,-~1., state's: "The first rule of all Contracts is "CLOSURE". There must be closure for the volition of the Contract, by the initiate. If there is a hidden meaning within ANY CONTRACT, and that meaning [Dictionary Term]was not advertised within that Contract and that meaning, was used for subversive or criminal activity, then that Contract falls under the terminology of, FRAUD." - (:Fraudulent-Parse-Syntax-Grammar.) / [syntax=parts of a word] -

CLOSURE: To provide a person (or position, office of importance) with factual information.

HISTORICAL CAVEAT:

2 NOV 1999: This was the day that all of the Federal Services being provided and overseen by Great Britain for the 50 Territories of the Union of the Republic - ("the united States of America" which operates under the Constitution **FOR THE** united States of America) - and the District of Columbia and its Federal Services Contract Corporation - (**"the United States of America inc."**, witch operates under the **Copyrighted** CORPORATE "copy-cat" Constitution **OF THE** United States of America inc.) - legally and lawfully ended and were dissolved.

(There are two completely separate Governments and two completely separate Government Systems. One is operating out of the District of Columbia in an effort to trick the other one by mirroring it in every manner, to confuse it, and eventually, assimilate it… in a long range Military Objective, to conquer it.) - Its the oldest trick in the book.

None-the-less, neither of those Documents are valid any longer. The Original Constitution "For the", was a Contract-Document between the king and the 13 Colonies, and that agreement ended 2 NOV 1999 when the king closed his Post Office in DC. **And the** Constitution "OF THE", was a "tweaked" COPY-CAT VERSION of the Original that was converted and "Copyrighted" by a PRIVATE FEDERAL

GOVERNMENT SERVICES CORPORATION, in an overall effort to confuse everyone with it,.. but it too,… along with the ORIGINAL, are both VOIDED.

Why, because the Americans no longer require a CONTRACT-DOCUMENT with Great Britain! - IT,.. IS,.. OVER! - THEY DO NOT REPRESENT US GLOBALLY ANY LONGER.

HOWEVER, THE DECLARATION of INDEPENDENCE & THE BILL OF RIGHTS,.. AND THE LIVING SPIRIT OF RESISTANCE AND FREEDOM THAT ETERNALLY RESIDES WITHIN THOSE DOCUMENTS, IS VISUALLY REPRESENTED BY THIS NATION'S IMMORTAL **TITLE: 4, American Federal Government (G-Spec) Flag, (OLD GLORY)** - THAT WILL NEVER DIE!!

This was Presidential Election year, and on the day, 2 NOV 1999 - **"the United States of America inc."**, (from here: **"the U.S.A. inc."**) due to the close of the 3 rd and final International bankruptcy, had to legally close the Post-Office in Washington DC down, and lawfully VACATE [End] the TRUST (Office of the President) and surrender it's private, CORPORATE Constitution and its authorizations validating its Standing as the International Federal Postal Services Provider (Office of the Postmaster General who authorizes our ability to conduct commerce with the rest of the world) for the 50 Territories and therefore, through this legal closing process, ceased to exist as the international representative & guardian in the affairs concerning all commerce globally for this nation.

In light of this legal information, it is BEYOND CLEAR that today, **"the U.S.A. inc."** is continuing to operate in an act of fraud well beyond its voided services agreement, as it has had no Legal/Lawful Federal Contracts in place and therefore no legal authorization or lawful standing to exist and/or operate whatsoever, anywhere within the 50 State Territories since, 2 NOV 1999; yet continues,..

(1) For 16 years, to pose and make-believe/masquerade as if it is still employed and representing the 50 united States of America in an International Federal capacity;

(2) for 16 years has continued VOID OF CONTRACT to beguile the 50 States and present fraudulently contrived illegal legislation and TYRANNICAL "executive orders" to the people of this Nation with no AUTHORIZATION, STANDING, or JURISDICTION to do so. All the while in a criminal process of deception, fraud, and Barra-try,... not to mention IMPERSONATING The POSTMASTER GEN-ERAL and the COMMANDER and CHIEF of a NATION; Branches of the Executors, Judicial and Legislative Officers and Personnel, respectively in a blatant Breach of Trust, Criminal Malfeasance and Embezzlement.

This list of illegal activity could easily keep running, but we will stop here, to conserve time and space.

2 NOV 1999 – Presidential Election Day in the United States. Remember the FLORIDA "CHADS"? - No one knew who won the election, Bush or Gore, because something had "happened" or "gone wrong" with the polling/voting box in Florida? And do you remember, that it took Florida exactly 90 days to "recount", the "votes"? -- Why is this important?

This is important because this was the end of the third and FINAL bankruptcy of "the United States of America Inc.". YES, INCOR-PORATED. That is the most important piece of our entire history; the fact that since after the American Revolutionary War, we have been little more than a Private Corporate Charter.

This is vital because, when the 13 Colonies won the War of Independence, more commonly known as the American Revolution, from Great Britain, those 13 Colonies were about to be invaded and taken over by another Monarch. In fact, there were two Monarchs that were arguing over who it would be to invade, and it all has to do with the POST OFFICE.

Now when the Colonies were first established, the Post-Office that they had in Philada, Pennsylvania, was overseen by **the Honourable Elliott Benger, Esquire; The Sole Deputy-Postmaster General of all, his Majesty's, Sovereign Lord George the Second King of Great Britain's, Dominions in America.**

Benjamin Franklin was appointed Postmaster of Philadelphia by the British Crown Postmaster General Elliott Benger in 1737. Postmaster General Elliott Benger then added to Franklin's duties by making him comptroller, with financial oversight for nearby Post Offices. Franklin lobbied the British to succeed Postmaster General Benger when his health failed and, with Virginia's William Hunter, was named Joint Postmaster General for the Crown on August 10, 1753. In 1764, Franklin returned to London, where he represented the interests of several colonial governments. But in 1774, judged too sympathetic to the colonies, he was dismissed as Joint Postmaster General for the British Crown.

However, One Year later back on American soil in 1775, Franklin served as a member of the Second Continental Congress, which appointed him Postmaster General for the united States of America, on July 26 of that year. [1775] With an annual salary of $1,000 and $340 for a secretary and comptroller. This postal position gave the 13 Colonies the standing/authorization to ship and receive mail,... [conduct commerce] vessels, cargo, and/or packages to and from, other postal locations on the planet. Not long after, the king tried to implement the Stamp Tax,.. remember? ...The king was told to get lost and shove it. - And then, he tried again later with the Tea Tax, responsible for the events of the Boston Tea-Party.

In 1776, Franklin worked with the committee that created the Declaration of Independence and eventually, the Colonies go to war in objection to a myriad of continued British intrusions and in so doing, had to close the Post Office of Benjamin Franklin down, because WAR VACATES ALL CONTRACT, and it was never reopened again. (This is extremely important)

Benjamin Franklin then left for Paris to secure French support for the war with England. When the American Revolution had come to an end, the Colonies were now in a state of bankruptcy. Owing 1.6 million franks to the French for funding the American Revolution, and a Nation in bankruptcy does not have the power to create, or enter into contract(s) (of any kind). Therefore, they were unable to procure and file their own contract to open a Post Office again after the war. A Post Office that would authorize them to conduct commerce and substantiate their newly acquired sovereign position, (National Contract Location) and as we all know, there are no free nations; as every other nation on the planet is ruled by some sort of Psychopathic Monarch or Dictator. As that is the case, none then, are truly free.

So then, Spain and France argued over who had first-right to invade to rape, steal, and plunder the New World and seize control of its natural resources. Spain insisting that Christopher Columbus had found and claimed it first, and France insisting that without their support and financial assistance this opportunity wouldn't even be available,.. plus they were owed 1.6mf. However, the king of Great Britain – still the king and the power in the world – slaps both down and instead, places his own Post Office up in the District of Columbia [a foreign enclave] in an effort to control, not only the shipping and receiving of everything moving in and/or out of the New World, [all commerce] but this Post Office granted the 13 Colonies with the Postal Authorizations needed as a Private Charter and now as a Franchise Corporate Extension of the District of Columbia's FEDERAL-POSTAL-CONTRACT- LOCATION, was authorized to conduct commerce with the rest of the Worlds Dictators and Monarchs.

Whom, if wanted to rape the New World of all of its natural resources, were going to have to contract with the king through his Post Office in DC to do so. Because – ONCE AGAIN - the treaty of alliance Benjamin Franklin negotiated in 1778 with the king of GB was vital to the success of the American Revolution. Later, Franklin helped negotiate the peace treaty "Treaty of Paris", with Great Britain and returned to Philadelphia in 1785. He attended the Constitutional Convention in 1787 and lived to see the Constitution adopted.

There was no Washington, DC until the United States Constitution was adopted 15, September 1787 which included **the authorization of the establishment of a Federal District.** When the United States Constitution was adopted on September 15, 1787, Article 1, Section 8, Clause 17, included language authorizing the establishment of a Federal District. This district was not to exceed 10 miles square, under the exclusive legislative authority of Congress. On July 16, 1790, Congress then authorized President George Washington to choose a permanent site for the capital city and, on December 1, 1800, the capital was moved from Philadelphia to an area along the Potomac River because of the ease of shipping the river allowed. (COMMERCE) He died Dec. 14, 1799.

June 11, 1878: In The Organic Act of 1878, Congress approves the establishment of the District of Columbia Government as a PRIVATE Municipal Government CORPORATION. (Just as he Tyrannically ruled the East Indies Trading Company, he now ruled America) and he got a nice piece of everyones pie in the process, as usual.. to say the least.

CONTINUING:

The First Objective of my Mission was to try and STOP A CIVIL WAR, by informing and EDUCATING the Public Civil Systems and their Municipalities on the MULTIPLE TYPES of FRAUD that have been played out against them, by the British Crown in the Crowns overall objective to eventually conquer us as a Nation,… which for me, was not going to be an easy task to tackle. But by the Grace of GOD, within 6 months I was directed to self appointed Common Law Judge, Anna-Von Reitz; who's personal mission it was to chronicle exactly that. Her entire account was filed with the Joint Chiefs of Staff, The Provost Marshal, The US MARSHALS, the FBI, and a myriad of other Agencies and Authorities of the highest order. All of this is in my initial 230-page Report to USSOCOM, titled; "HARVESTED". – Here is a recap that brings you up to current speed on what Rothschild has just done to try and solidify the ILLE-GAL, "Surrender and Capture" of this Nation.

... A Nation on a Continent that he god-damned knows Good & Well, belongs to :POSTMASTER- GENERAL, FEDERAL-POSTAL-JUDGE, COMMANDER-AND-CHIEF :Russell-Jay: Gould.

I am injecting a small section of my first Report, titled; - "The Assessment" into this report in an effort to bring you up to speed. The historical outline provided was written by Judge Anna-Von Reitz, who although, does know who :FEDERAL-POSTAL-JUDGE :David-Wynn: Miller is, but whom has no knowledge, or understanding for what :POSTMASTER-GENERAL, FEDERAL-POSTAL-JUDGE, COMMANDER-AND-CHIEF :Russell-Jay: Gould has done, that FEDERAL-POSTAL-JUDGE :David-Wynn: Miller participated with him in as his witness, and his assistant, and whom is also his Corporate-Quantum-Global-Government-Partner of THE UNITY-STATES OF OUR WORLD-CORPORATION.

EVIDENCE: Annex ~1-A

SECTION OF MY FIRST MISSION REPORT

FINAL REPORT
- THE ASSESSMENT -

1 OCT 2015

FOR THE ATTENTION OF: *US ARMY - SPECIAL OPERATIONS FORCES / 1 st, 3 rd, 5 th, 7 th, 10 th, 11 th, 20 th SF GROUPS / 75 th RANGERS / 160 th SOAR / USACAPOC / US NAVY SEALS / MARSOC / US SPECIAL OPERATIONS COMMAND*

SUBJECT: *The Orchestrated take-down of, "the united States of America"*

CLASSIFICATION: *: Op-Sec Level (N/A)*

: DEF CON 2
: URGENT
: UNCLASSIFIED
: FORCEPRO INITIATED

HARVESTED TO DEATH: *- Final Report and Assessment -*

Investigation conducted by:
***FORMER: US ARMY SPECIAL OPERATIONS FORCES TEAM-LEADER/
MEMBER PSYCHOLOGICAL OPERATIONS SPECIALIST /
USACAPOC / USSOCOM***

(Report: by Anna-Von Reitz)

What does this mean?

It means we have been defrauded by international banking cartels operating "governmental services corporations" as if these entities were our lawful government. It means that the Holy See and the British Monarch have acted in secretive Breach of Trust and Dishonor and have undermined our rightful government since 1845. It means that we have caught the rats red-handed, proved the facts, and demanded remedy.

FRANCISCUS, the dba name of the Pope, issued his Motu Proprio and made the members of the Bar Associations responsible for their errors and omissions. This effectively washed his hands of the criminality of the Bar Members and the continuing assaults upon us by the British Crown and ended their privateer licenses and other protections that had been extended to them in Breach of Trust. So far, so good.

(NOTE: Anna-Von Reitz, (God bless her) has no idea that there is NO SUCH THING, as FRANCISCUS, dba "the Pope", or whatever he wants to call himself and PRETEND TO BE, or FICTIONALLY CLAIM that he is... WHATEVER. - ITS ALL FAKE and a FRAUD. Also to be explained later in this report.)

However, there has been no action to dismantle the mechanisms of the fraud that has been practiced against the living people. Every day, babies are born in hospitals and are "registered" as chattel belonging to privately owned and operated corporations masquerading as our government. These corporations patent and trademark our bodies and our names and create "citizens" for themselves that they ultimately control as slaves. This practice of "enslavement by proxy" is no less repugnant than physical enslavement and it has the same results.

They have accomplished this by obtaining undisclosed contracts under conditions of coercion and misrepresentation and by blatant fraud upon the probate courts and falsification of the civil records. They have had each one of us declared "legally dead"---- "Missing, presumed lost at sea"---and have seized upon our estates as presumed secondary beneficiaries. This legal chicanery has been assisted and expedited by a few evil politicians who literally conspired to sell their countrymen into slavery for profit.

They seize upon our property by presuming that it is "abandoned". This is what has happened to every so-called "mortgage payment" you have ever made. It has been seized by the banks as abandoned property belonging to your own estate. They take title to our land, homes, businesses, and other private property and public property interests under color of law. They disguise installment leases as "land sales". They disguise repurchase agreements as "loans". They disguise "security notes" as "promissory notes". And they steal us blind, taking their pay out of our treasury and otherwise using and abusing our own assets to do it.

Just as they have seized upon our private property via a process of fraud and deceit, they have attempted to seize upon our entire nation and claim that it is "abandoned property". To understand how this works you have to understand the first frauds committed against us, for it is in the beginning that we most clearly see the ends.

1. March 27, 1861, the actual elected Congress ceases to function.
2. Lincoln creates a corporation doing business as "The United States of America inc." and uses what is left of the Congress as a Board of Directors.
3. This "Corporate Congress" changes the meaning of the word "person" to mean "corporation" for their own private in-house corporate purposes. (37th Congress, Second Session, Chapter 49, Section 68).
4. The Corporate Congress changes the meaning of more words--- according to them, the meaning of the words "state", "State" and "United States" all magically mean ""the territories and the District of Columbia" (13 Stat. 223, 306, ch. 173, sec. 182, June 30, 1864.)
5. These "special definitions" adopted by "a" Congress operating a private, for-profit corporation doing business as "The United States of America" then secretly allowed the rats to "presume" that anyone who used the common meaning of these words and admitted to living in a "state" or the "United States" was submitting to be considered and treated as a "citizen" of the District of Columbia, instead. In their secretively altered lexicon, "United States Citizen = District of Columbia Citizen"

June 11, 1878: In The Organic Act of 1878, Congress approves the establishment of the District of Columbia Government as a PRIVATE Municipal Government Corporation.

6. And as anyone reading The Constitution can see, this meant submitting to the rule of "Congress" which was given plenary control of the District of Columbia. Via the use of semantic deceit a small group of venal criminals "redefined" our Republic as a plenary oligarchy run by none other than themselves. They also endeavored to redefine all the freeborn Americans as slaves belonging to the District of Columbia. Never mind that the "Congress" engaging in this fraud and merely pretending to be the lawfully elected Congress had

28

absolutely no public office and no delegated authority.

7. What happened with all this fraud by a hundred years later? The Congressional Record, June 13, 1967, pp. 15641-15646 - "A 'citize of the United States is a civilly dead entity operating as a co-trustee and co-beneficiary of the PCT, the private constructive, cestui que trust of US Inc. under the 14th Amendment, which upholds the debt of the USA and US Inc. in Section 4."

Now, put all this together in one big Ball of Wax, and what do you get?

The Bar Association Members employed by the District of Columbia Municipal Corporation have been "presuming" that you are "civilly dead" because you have been falsely reported as "missing, presumed dead" on the records of their probate courts. While they have been busily and secretively "presuming" this, they have also been "presuming" that you died intestate (without a Will) and that the local District of Columbia Municipal Corporation franchise doing business as (for example) the STATE OF OKLAHOMA, is the beneficiary of all your property.

How's that for a fraud racket? How's that for conflict of interest?

But they didn't stop there. They also presume that the still living man is a "co-trustee" and "co- beneficiary" of his own estate trust. How can that be? Obviously, he can't be the trustee AND the beneficiary of his own estate at the same time, because the two roles are mutually exclusive. So they send out a false summons to you as the "presumed" co-trustee of the JOHN QUINCY ADAMS estate trust, and you, ignorantly assuming that this is your name and that this mail is addressed to you, show up in answer to their "summons"---- and they trick you into playing the role of trustee, while they suck up the beneficiary slot and milk your estate.

That is what these demons in suits have been playing at all these years. They charge your estate millions of dollars for every "felony" charge they utter and nearly as much for every "misdemeanor". Then for good measure, they throw you in jail and make the taxpayers pay a hundred times more than any real cost for the "service" of incarcerating you----and profiting off your labor in "prison industries". They bilk billions of dollars out of the public treasury and out of your private "abandoned" estates every year, while parading around the town as members of "elite" society.

(This is a NATIONAL-SECURITY-ALERT: Common Law Courts, for the mot part, have been deceptively transitioned by this long-range-objective into "Federal Corporate Courts", wherein people are illegally punished and extorted by this foreign and domestic enemy as clearly identified as such, in Article One of the Constitution. All Attorneys are Foreign Citizens to the united States by Constitutional Law. This entire construct of Codes and Statutes must be arrested and ended in the name of NATIONAL-SECURITY, WITHOUT DELAY.) -

No doubt the word "elite" has also been redefined by these maggots to mean "common criminal". There is no doubt now that this system is what it is, nor is there any doubt that it must end, but before we leave this subject, please note, that they haven't been content with defrauding, press-ganging, enslaving, and taxing you under false pretenses, oh, no, they finally maxed out your credit cards which they stole along with your identity as a living breathing man.

So the Big Game has been afoot: do the same thing we did to each one of the people to the entire nation.

How do we do that?

November 7, 2007 the rats in Washington, DC running the "United States, Inc." bankrupted it for the third and final time. They handed it over to the UN to act as bankruptcy trustee and nobody named a successor to The Constitution contract.

(NOTE: - HERE IS THE ILLEGAL TAKEOVER and SURRENDER of The United States of America, RIGHT IN FRONT OF YOUR

30

FACE. However, there is more than one "United States", but the date she references is erroneous in some regard, and again she demonstrates that she knows NOTHING in relation to what COMMANDER :Gould: has accomplished. -)

That left the "Federal" side of the Constitution contract flapping in the wind, and the United Nations Trust Committee -- North America overseeing our National Trust assets, and no other entity named to provide the nineteen enumerated services that the British-controlled Federal United States is supposed to provide.

(NOTE: - THIS IS WHERE "Judge" Anna-Von Reitz, IS ABSOLUTELY WRONG, and had NO CLUE UNTIL I CONTACTED HER and INFORMED HER as to WHAT IT IS THAT :POSTMASTER-GENERAL, FEDERAL-POSTAL-JUDGE, COMMANDER-AND-CHIEF :Russell-Jay: Gould, and :FEDERAL-POSTAL-JUDGE :David-Wynn: Miller, have done for America and "For We the People", of this great Nation to end and disqualify all of this illegal nonsense. Her Mission now, should she decide to take it has been to now inform America of the FACTS, in relation to the contents of this report.)

Nice.

Last week, the infernal bastards (Rothschild) filed a claim on abandonment against our entire nation, claiming that we no longer exist as a sovereign nation because we haven't been heard from in 150 years. They further claimed that we are no longer a sovereign nation because we (allegedly) don't have a national currency in circulation.

We had to file a Declaration of Joint Sovereignty and two new sets of Sovereign Letters Patent to rebut their unending "presumptions" before the UN Trust Committee- North America and the UN Security Council.

The fact is that we are sovereigns in joint tenancy; if we don't attend to our business in a hundred years, it's still our business. If we don't call a Continental Convention in 200 years, that's our business, too. And we are not obligated to have a national currency in circulation---even though we do.

It's the same schtick they are trying to pull only on a much larger scale--- claiming that our whole nation is effectively "missing, presumed lost" and that our estate is "abandoned" ready for the taking by secondary beneficiaries and creditors.

That's what the banks and their buddies the lawyers and their flunkies the politicians you elected in good faith had planned for you.

That's what Wells Fargo Bank---- which is not a bank----it's a "securities investment corporation" using the trademarked name "Wells Fargo Bank" to pretend that its a bank---has been trying to promote this past week. And no wonder. It is partially owned and operated by the "US Attorney General".

And now, let's make it Perfectly Clear---- General Dunsford, you are responsible for providing for the security of the American People. You receive your paycheck directly or indirectly from funds and credit obtained from us - (ACTUALLY THEY ARE PAID BY THE IMF, Rothschild) - even if it is now in the hands of pirates and brigands and those who have colluded with them as false trustees. These evil men and women would like to start a Civil War in America, because they make their money off of conflict.

In preparation for trying to incite an uprising – (RACE WAR/WAR OF ANY KIND) - among the peaceful American people these criminals have armed corporate subcontractors that are operating under names designed to make people assume they are lawful units of government---- BATF, FEMA, IRS, DHS, FBI, CIA, local "Sheriffs" who are nothing but shills working in private corporate offices, not Sheriffs occupying public offices on the land at all ---- and have armed these private commercial mercenaries with billions of rounds of ammunition and tactical weapons. For what purpose?

(NOTE: - THEY DON'T KNOW THAT, :POSTMASTER-GEN-ERAL :Russell-Jay: Gould, IS THEIR NEW POSTMASTER, and they DO NOT KNOW THAT THEY ARE BEING USED TO DE-STROY THEIR OWN NATION –- This is the POTENTIAL CIVIL WAR that I AM TRYING TO STOP WITH THE INFORMATION CONTAINED WITHIN THIS REPORT!)

So that the secondary creditors of a bankruptcy that we were never legitimately any part of ---international banking cartels and foreign investors---can come in here and loot and pillage America with the assistance of commercial mercenaries bought and paid for with ille-gal taxes extorted from Americans by criminals pretending to be our lawful government. -

END REPORT CAVEAT -

** THIS, has been the overall family objective of the entire
Royal British Crown. **

CONTINUING -

LONG STORY SHORT – Due to particular banking laws, a Nation is only to be allowed 3 international bankruptcies before itself, stands in a position ready to be captured/seized, and where its Nation's Government is taken over by a Monarch. This is the king's age old system of Feudalism (Feudalistic Warfare) that the monarch's and dictator's of the world have used to conquer everything and every-one, over the eons.

BIG NEWS: - 2 NOV 1999, due to INTERNATIONAL BANKING LAW, the king of Great Britain had to legally close his Post Office in the District of Columbia down and VACATE THE TRUST. – (which is the Office of the President) – [i.e. the Contracted Middle-Man between the US and GB] Congress was also closed and ended, and so was the Senate.

IT WAS OFFICIALLY OVER. The "Bank-Note" Contract, which was "THE US CONSTITUTION" (kings government) and the "BILL

OF RIGHTS" (Peoples protection against the kings over intrusive government) and the Accord, "Joinder" between the two, HAD OFFICIALLY COME TO AN END.

So why did it take 90-days for Florida to re-count the votes between Bush and Gore? The fake "recount" was to distract the DUMBED DOWN and UNEDUCATED MASSES of, not only America, but all of the people of the world, and **because NOTHING becomes law for 90 days after your 3 rd and final bankruptcy.** Therefore everyone needed to be distracted so as not to notice that for 90 days, there was no Congress, Senate, IRS,... Nothing,... it was all closed down. [Managed, like Sheeple] So at the end of those 90-days, they announced that George Bush was appointed [by GB, the IMF/WORLD BANK & the VATICAN] (not elected – unbeknownst to the people) as the first President and CEO, of the new CORPORATE AMERICA. – The Font Style, Grammar, Punctuation, etc.. of the name, "The United States of America inc.", is the most important thing to take notice of in the changing of the name, for the People's Government, as the 3 bankruptcies had each come to an end.

The name was changed subtly each time to obfuscate the fraud they were once again going to re-initiate against the people, under – WHAT THE PEOPLE THOUGHT – was their own Government, simply because it was pronounced the same. But what they failed to recognize, due to a lack of awareness and education, was that the Grammatical Punctuation had been purposefully changed. Thereby – and unbeknown to the people – a new government had actually been created and had taken control of the Government System for them, to once again use the very same system, with the same sounding name, to initiate another round of the same game of grammar and bank-fraud. However, as we all know, any one or thing, although sounding the same, yet spelled differently are in fact, two separate and completely different entities altogether. This act of grammar and bank-fraud had been conducted against this Nation three times, and each time, the spelling, [syntax] had been changed. As is clearly obvious under closer observation, and when you look at the 3 independent Spellings of this Nation [Grammatical Construct] each time that it had changed hands, you will see what I mean.

EXAMPLE: "the United States inc." – "The UNITED STATES INC." - etc..

NOW, HERE IS WHERE THIS STORY GETS REALLY JUICY AND THIS IS WHERE AMERICA WAS SET FREE FROM THE TYRANNY IN "the District of Columbia"... YET IT IS BEING WITHHELD FROM THE WHOLE WORLD.

WHAT EVERYONE IS BEING LED TO BELIEVE [sheeple] is that on 2 NOV 1999, when the king had to VACATE and close his Post Office in DC, it ended all commerce on this planet between the U.S. and anyone they were contracted to conduct commerce with. And since we were still bankrupt (owing 12-Trillion to IMF/WB?) and unable to substantiate our national independent standing with a POSTAL-CONTRACT-LOCATION-DOCUMENT of our own, conducting commerce would be impossible, as it would be for any Nation.

So at this point, the United States of America was to be secretly SURRENDERED back over into the hands of the king of GB, as the Nation was now just CAPTURED by the kings age old system of feudalistic warfare via, The IMF/WORLD BANK. [a.k.a. the Rothschild's] - AND ALL OF IT, BY GRAND DESIGN.

The king, is of course the TRUST and could have paid, or waved the debt off, had he so chosen to do so, but the real long-range-objective of his plan was to CAPTURE the country, not allow it to remain free. This is why they - " His Federal Employees in Washington DC." - now hang the US Flag pointed down in a SURRENDERED POSITION; and this is also why you are witnessing the FOREIGN and OPPRESSIVE POWER of the BRITISH-RUN FEDERAL GOVERNMENT [kings government] being forced down and upon and into the States to the DETRIMENT of the States themselves and the people of this once great nation.

-And they, **"the Empire of the 3 City States"**, has secretly been behind, and at the heart of the illegal takeover and surrender of this country – not only since the time it was founded – but more precisely, within the last 16 years. Operating openly and blatantly without fear of reprisal from anyone, they fear nothing. Which is why Obama Bin Ladin has been recorded and heard to say, *"The American people need to shut the fuck up, I'm a king."* - and continues unimpeded by any one, or any power, as he drafts absolutely illegal laws in an act of fraud that LITERALLY do nothing less than bind everyone and everything under the rule of those drunken, illegal, fraudulent, FICTION decrees. FICTION Decrees that are passed off to the mundane as "Mandates", "Executive Orders" (as if such a thing could ever exist) or "law(s)". Talk about a joke. - This is why they want your guns. THEY FEAR THAT YOU WILL COME TO KNOW THE TRUTH CONTAINED WITHIN THIS DOCUMENT, AND RISE UP AGAINST THEM; and that is what they fear the most.

NOW, FOR THE REAL SURPRISE,.. AND THE TRUTH!

HOWEVER, despite that you're being told [or not] that this Nation has been surrendered back over and into the hands of a Monarch; that you are Peasants, Slaves & Surfs; you have no Military, No Country, No Flag, No National Standing and therefore, No Authorization to exist as a nation of people,..

THE ACTUAL, AND TRUTHFUL FACT OF THIS ENTIRE MATTER IS THAT, on 2 NOV 1999, when the king closed his Post Office in the District of Columbia down, and VACATED and SURRENDERED the TRUST, he was back-doored by a REAL AMERICAN named, :Russell-Jay: Gould. Who had foreseen the close of the kings Post Office coming, and secretly legged himself, and his entire global government construct, into that now, newly VACANT and ABANDONED location, as the NEW POSTMASTER-GENERAL for the United States of America.

He did this by prepositioning himself and waiting for the 2000 Florida

CHADS to play out. This involved the king having to wait for them as well, which was too long, thereby VIOLATING - (TITLE 39, sec. 101 / and TITLE: 15, 2301, Document Time lines – lost continuance) - MAKING THE WHOLE ELECTIONS PROCESS ILLEGAL! Because the United States NO LONGER NEEDED A MIDDLEMAN (President) BETWEEN US and Great Britain and the Post Office because the Contract Legally had come to an end.

So when the king Legally and Lawfully VACATED the TRUST, (Office of the President) the OFFICE of the POSTMASTER GENERAL, and lost Command and Control of the Military, (controlled by the Postmaster),… he was back doored on 8 JULY 2000, by a FACTUAL American, named :Russell-Jay: Gould. Wherewith, :Russell-Jay: Gould's bonafied, certified "Bills of the Lading's" (Certification) for that position, on 8 JULY 2000, kicked in. Bills of the Lading's, which were the Certification-Documents that Legally VALIDATED the Authorization of his LAWFUL STANDING as the new POSTMASTER-GENERAL in the District of Columbia, for the United States of America.

Thereby, in doing so, kept the continuance of the evidence of the POST-OFFICE for this nation open, and in play around the world. Wherewith, his POSTAL-COMMAND-CONTRACT-LOCATION-FILING being recognized by every other global leader in the world, he then heroically stopped the illegal takeover and surrender of this great nation by disqualifying the fraudulently conveyed Bankruptcy Note of the IMF, and further authorized the continuity of all commerce on Planet Earth between the 50 States of this Nation and whomever they were contracted, and had contracts with, to continue to conduct that commerce. [shipment(s) and movement(s) of everything; from money, to people.]

THIS IS SO POWERFUL THAT IT MUST BE DESCRIBED IN GREAT DETAIL TO BE BOTH FULLY UNDERSTOOD AND APPRECIATED, OR ELSE YOU WILL NEVER COME TO GRASP THE FULL MAGNITUDE OF SUCH AN ALL ENCOMPASSING GLOBAL EVENT THAT LITERALLY CHANGED THE

BALANCE OF POWER ON THIS ENTIRE PLANET BY TAK-
ING IT FROM THE CORRUPTED DESPOTS WHO WERE US-
ING IT TO CONQUER THIS ROCK IN SPACE, AND PLACED IT
ALL,.. ALL OF IT,.. AND I MEAN EVERY LAST BIT OF IT, BACK
INTO THE HANDS OF GOD, and therefor "We the People", YOU!
- FOREVER.

The fact is, THE DECLARATION OF INDEPENDENCE has
NEVER EXPIRED and is still very much IN EFFECT just as much
as it was, the day that it was drafted. However, the "Original U.S.
Constitution" (it pains me to say) was a "Bank-Note" and an "Accord" struck between the 13 Colonies and the king of GB. Whom
was ultimately chosen by the founders of the Republic as the Monarch that they were willing to sign an International Postal Contract
with, rather than suffer at the hands of one of the other two, of whom
they had never known the tyrannies of.

The "Bill of Rights" is a simple DEFENSE LIST of the TOP 10
THINGS (Amongst others) that the 13 Colonies made sure were
CLEARLY RECOGNIZED by the king as HUMAN FREEDOMS
and/or PERSONAL ITEMS/EQUIPMENT THAT WERE COM-
PLETELY OUT OF HIS ABSOLUTE COMMAND AND/OR CON-
TROL OF. And as he did not write the "Bill of Rights", he therefore
has NO AUTHORIZATION [Authority] or STANDING WHATSO-
EVER, TO QUESTION, CONTEST, and/or ALTER or RENOUNCE
that list in any way, shape, or form, and never has.

A SOLDIERS PERSPECTIVE

Now, as we think about what all of this means, and seriously take a
good long hard look at what in the hell is going on in our country, the
events that are outlined and detailed within this report, will give you
an understanding for what is going on, that you would have never
had, otherwise.

When you step back and examine this situation, you can see that the
Private Federal Government Services Corporation, **"the United**

States of America inc." seems to legitimately be going forward and along with the FICTION BANKRUPTCY, SURRENDER and TAKE-OVER of this entire nation, as if what :FEDERAL-POSTAL-JUDGE :Russell-Jay: Gould, had never happened and as though they think
that they have the consent of the people and the people's entire Military at their back to allow them to do so.

Please understand - IF, our country has been found and declared to be derelict in its obligatory responsibility, in good faith, to honor its financial agreements with the IMF and the WORLD BANK, (Rothschild) and/or, the FEDERAL RESERVE, et. al, and therefore we have been dissolved as a nation,… and our founding document-contracts (Declaration, Bill of Rights, etc..) have been nullified, and are gone, because the US Constitution was nothing more than a BANK-NOTE, then that is to say that, there is NO MORE United States of America. It is further to say, that all of the States have been dissolved, along with their State Governments and all of their State Civil Systems, along with all Civil Authority to include the Legislative and Judicial Branches founded and based upon the 10 Commandments of GOD and the Gospel Truths and Pure Doctrines of our Christian form of American Government .

Furthermore, as there is NO Declaration of Independence, NO US Constitution, and NO Bill of Rights, then there are NO LAWS AT ALL and NO CIVIL SYSTEM OF ANY AUTHORITY, that has the power to enforce any form of Civil Obedience whatsoever. And if our country has been surrendered back over into the hands of a Monarch by Agents of the IMF, and our Flag has also been surrendered as well; and the land of the country was captured by this takeover and surrendered, then we have no country to call our Home; and are no longer even considered Americans because we have no Nation as a people, and therefore NO LAND to call our Country to even exist upon; Where our Nation's Military, has no Flag to muster itself under in Declaration of our National Standing; National Standing that authorizes the recognition of our Defensive Authority in protection of our Country and our Flag, and ultimately in Defense and protection of our Country and our Flag, and ultimately in Defense and protection of our way of life and finally in the continued Defense and Protection of every last GOD Given Freedom afforded to evey man, woman and child in this Nation. that GOD Himself has given them!

IF, our Country has been surrendered and captured – which is exactly what they say has happened and what is clearly going on around us – then our Nations Military Members would therefore be little more than a Rogue Industrial Military Complex for hire, and nothing more than Homeless, Wayward Warrior Mercenaries; without a Country, a Flag, or a Nation of their own to defend, or to call,… home.

That is a logical conclusion as to why our Soldiers are being charged with murder when they shoot someone on the battle-field. They are nothing more than hired guns and clubs; "Mercenaries". And if you are nothing more than a hired contract killer (Mercenary) it would only make sense that if you shot and killed someone you would be charged for murder. And as hired killers, they are not on a battle-field of any kind, as they are not Soldiers from a legitimate Country to substantiate their standing to constitute a declaration of war on their part from.

This is a lot to psychologically deal with and contemplate as a US Armed Forces Soldier, let alone a Special Operations Soldier, to say the least. Here this whole time, we have thought that we were defending our Nation and our Country from some downtrodden and financially deprived 3 rd World Terrorists Organizations riding around on camels, and come to find out, we have unknowingly been being used and are in the Command and Control of the very Organization that just engineered our own Country's absolute destruction.

The gravity of this information, when seriously and fully contemplated is catastrophic to say the least. The magnitude of such a reality, for most, could have never even been conceived, let alone contemplated to be countered and therefore, thought to be stopped.

:**Disclaimer** – The timetable(s) associated with the events that took place and are relayed within this report, are not in the actual chronicled order that they factually took place in, but are altered for the purpose of simplifying what happened, and is done in an effort to not complicate the story.

BUT THANK GOD IT WAS.

Since that historic day 2 NOV 1999, when the king legally and lawfully closed his Post Office down in Washington DC [District of Columbia – a Foreign Enclave and Private Corporate City-State] and VACATED the TRUST, (Office of the President/Middleman) the United States of America has had a new Sovereign Ruler by his own right, and by his own globally recognized, Global Government System, leg his GLOBAL-FEDERAL-POSTAL-CONTRACT-AUTHORIZATION'S in at that now abandoned, FEDERAL-POSTAL-CONTRACT-LOCATION for the United States, as the new POSTMASTER-GENERAL for the country. In so-doing, on 8 JULY 2000 he assumed the Position of the TRUST for this Nation, assuming the "Bankruptcy Note", (stopping the surrender of this Nation and the surrender of its Flag) kept the continuance of the evidence for the Federal Post Office of the District of Columbia in play, as well as in good global standing and authorized the Nation to continue its Commerce Globally with the rest of the world.

After this Earth Shattering Event had taken place, what this MONUMENTAL MOVE had just done, was finalize the legal and lawful end of the king of Great Britain's Federal Postal Authorization's (Command & Control of Commerce) for the 13 Colonies, and now 50 States of the Union of the Republic, and further, as that Federal-Postal-Contract-Location was just taken over, it closed all of the Courts (Court Houses) across the Nation, down for good. Courts on American Soil that were long since overtaken by the kings OUT-

LAWED, FOREIGN and DOMESTIC ENEMY, Court System (identified within the Declaration of Independence) that were now running and operating on, and under, International Admiralty and Maritime Law of the Sea, and therefore out of their Jurisdiction. -

How? – Those locations are registered and identified as "VESSELS IN DRY-DOCK" [BOATS] by the Port Authorities that are sitting and operating within your States Territories. When you are beaten down and drug into those foreign locations "Vessels in Dry-Dock", [BOATS] that, unbeknownst to you, belong to the king, against your will, you are illegally charged and arraigned under duress, and extorted by "Codes & Statutes" of a Foreign and Domestic Enemy System and Court to this nation. (identified in the Declaration of Independence) After which, or in addition to being extorted, you are then thrown into a box by the king,.. AND HIS MEN. Whom, unbeknownst to the American COP'S, are IN-FACT, the American COPS, themselves. [Undereducated Americans] Literally tearing their own country apart.

This also solidified the close and the official end of Congress, to include the Senate. Greater still, it officially signified THE END of the BIRTH-CERTIFICATE SYSTEM that was initiated to ENSLAVE and ensure the COLLECTION OF TAXES in an effort to create WEALTH for the "Royal Family's", which was further enforced by the NOW DISQUALIFIED and OFFICIALLY CLOSED, Internal Revenue Service, (IRS).

Ultimately, and the Coupe-De'Gras of this entire take-down, and what this means to America and every single American, is this… Since the end of the American Revolutionary War, the 13 Colonies and the now 50 Sovereign, Independent Nation-States and their sovereign independent forms of Government, that had come together under GOD, and gathered themselves under the Flag of this Nation, to form a more perfect Federal Union of the Republic of the United States of America, have always been little more than a Private Charter beholden to a Contract Bank-Note, as a Franchise Extension of a Global Corporation, UNTIL NOW.

42

This beautiful Country, that we have all been taught and have come to know as an Independent and Sovereign Nation, was in reality, never a NATION, OR FREE, OR SOVEREIGN. it was simply little more than a Private Charter beholden to a Bank-Note and incorporated as a Franchise Extension of the crown, that was opened up and allowed to conduct Commerce with the rest of the world through the kings postal location in the District of Columbia, in an effort to eventually destroy, capture, and finally surrender it. JUST AS IS SECRETLY and ILLEGALLY BEING DONE RIGHT NOW, and RIGHT BEFORE OUR VERY SLEEPY, UNEDUCATED EYES.

WHAT you are NOT BEING TOLD, is the FACT that this Nation has a new POSTMASTER-GENERAL, and his name is :POSTMASTER-GENERAL, FEDERAL-POSTAL-JUDGE :Russell-Jay: Gould,… and he's an American.

A VERY POWERFUL and SMALL GLOBALLY ELITE GROUP of individuals operating and holding positions at the highest levels of Government, occupying military seats around the world, including Rulers of the United Nations, The PENTAGON, the VATICAN and their Sitting BLACK-POPE and JESUIT GENERAL, to especially include THE ROYAL FAMILIES themselves, are the only ones that have any idea what in the hell just happened here in the United States and just how huge what POSTMASTER-GENERAL, FEDERAL-POSTAL-JUDGE :Russell-Jay: Gould, has just accomplished, is.

EVEN WORSE YET, is that this Elite Group is now ILLEGALLY using the Quantum Authorizations of the very Quantum System that was created by :POSTMASTER-GENERAL, FEDERAL-POSTAL-JUDGE :Russell-Jay: Gould, and that LITERALLY took them down and destroyed them, to their advantage in both directions against everyone they owe money to. As if its some great new game that they get to play called, "Hey, lets use this to F*** everyone". Wherein what they are doing is, what they've always done,… Nothing. They say the Contracts are in Fiction so, we don't have to honor them, and vice-versa', its a Fact Contract, so its not a game of crime, so… we don't play..

43

IN ORDER TO FULLY COMPREHEND, exactly who FEDERAL-POSTAL-JUDGE & :POSTMASTER-GENERAL :Russell-Jay: Gould is, can be understood in knowing and realizing that he is a Sovereign Global Commander and Chief by his own right and the ruler of his own Global System of Government IN CORRECTNESS. The Titles and Global Authorizations associated with these positions are fully recognized by the United Nations, the Vatican, the Pentagon and London City, (The Empire of the 3 City-States) and he is vested with all the power and global authorizations to exercise the authorities associated with those positions as the Global Commander and Chief that he is.

Therefore what he has done by taking command and control of the Post Office in Washington DC – as a SOVEREIGN RULER and GLOBAL COMMANDER and CHIEF of HIS OWN GLOBAL GOVERNMENT SYSTEM is end the reign of tyranny that has plagued this country in the form of oppressive taxes and human abuses that have always been illegal in both the eyes of GOD and Man, by nullifying every last one of them with extreme prejudice. None of them are valid as they have no standing or authorization to exist. To especially include those introduced and enacted within the last 16 years straight.

What he has further done is become the FIRST PERSON IN THE WORLD to establish himself as a SOVEREIGN RULER of his own Global Government System. He is also the first person to use that authority to take command and control of a Foreign Enclave that was once the Federally Contracted Global Postal Location of his native nations tyrannical Monarchy away from that Monarch. He is also the first person to ever capture a Monarch's FEDERAL-POSTAL-CONTRACT-LOCATION and Foreign Enclave, to heroically take control of it, in an effort to save his nation from an illegal takeover and fraudulent surrender back into the hands of that Monarch, that the people of his native nation had never even seen coming.

How then, was the long-range plan by Great Britain to surrender this nation and take it over through the banking operations of the IMF/ WORLD BANK, stopped?

FOR ONE, they were stopped when :FEDERAL-POSTAL-JUDGE and POSTMASTER-GENERAL :Russell-Jay: Gould, assumed full responsibility as the Trust for this Nation as its new POSTMAS-TER-GENERAL and further proceeded to Legally and Lawfully disqualify, and nullify any and all banking "Notes" and/or "Monetary Transactions" ever conducted between the United States and the IMF/ WORLD BANK, as Contract-Grammar and Bank-Fraud. Whereby under these TITLES and amongst many other charges, he set the entire Nation free again from every Law ever enACTED. -

~TITLE~18: USCS~1001 &~1002: "Fictitious Conveyance of Grammar"

~TITLE~15: USCS~1692 E "False and Misleading Statements"

~TITLE~18: USCS~241: "Criminal-Conspiracy" = Tort

~TITLE~18: USCS~1512: "Obstruction of the Law" :AILING = CORRUPTION AT THE START/BEGINNING

(Just to list a few)

The intellectual understanding for the many Administrative moves that were needed and were correctly preformed in order and in conjunction, almost simultaneously one with the other, allowed many moves to be successfully accomplished that could have by no other means taken place whatsoever independently, as each move was made to support and substantiate the standing and the authorizations of the other.

In correlation to these standings, multiple authorizations were obtained and with that, :FEDERAL-POSTAL-JUDGE, POSTMAS-TER-GENERAL :Russell-Jay: Gould, then asked the Pentagon if they had an official Copyright and/or a Patent for the TITLE 4;

1 x 1.9 dimension Federal Flag (G-Spec; Government Flag) of the United States of America? – Interestingly enough, they had never been asked that before, nor did any such documents exist to support, nor substantiate its existence or its standing in relation to whom it represented or to whom its command and control of was officially even allocated to. At this point the question to the Pentagon was moot, as :Russell, had already filed for both a Patent and a Copyright before he had even approached the Pentagon; knowing that they did not have one. He therefore presented them with the CORRECT-LE-GAL-FILINGS for ownership of the - now captured – Federal Flag for this Nation, of which – TO THEIR GREAT SURPRISE - he was now THE LEGAL and LAWFUL, :POSTMASTER-GENERAL and COMMANDER-AND-CHIEF - The Pentagon knows this, and is very aware of the fact that what you are reading here, is absolutely true.

With LEGAL OWNERSHIP and LAWFUL-TACTICAL-COM-MAND-AND-CONTROL of the TITLE 4: Federal Flag of the United States of America in his possession, and having LEGALLY and LAWFULLY CAPTURED the LEGALLY & LAWFULLY VA-CATED BRITISH-FEDERAL-POSTAL-LOCATION up in Washington DC, :POSTMASTER-GENERAL, COMMANDER-AND-CHIEF, :Russell-Jay: Gould, in a heroic effort to save his Nation from a FRAUDULENT and ILLEGAL, SURRENDER and CAP-TURE [Takeover] by the BRITISH Crown, literally risked his own physical life and the lives of his entire family, to take the Empire of the 3 City States on.

:FEDERAL-POSTAL-JUDGE, POSTMASTER-GENERAL & :COMMANDER-AND-CHIEF :Russell-Jay :Gould, accompanied by :FEDERAL-POSTAL-JUDGE :David-Wynn: Miller, then re-opened the actual Benjamin Franklin Post Office in Philadelphia, Pennsylvania. The big secret in relation to this Post Office is that, not only is it a Historical Landmark & National Treasure, but it's the Nation's Original-Nativity-Location, where the founding of the Origi-nal Government of the united States of America was conceptualized. But what is not known is that the Post-Command-Authorizations that are attributed to that Postal-Command-Contract-Location are actually identified with the existence of the Benjamin Franklin Post-Office Building. The Authorizations that substantiate its Standing and recognition as a COMMAND-POST are granted within its Secret Architectural Masonic construction and by the layout, or order of decorum, identified within the POST OFFICE, itself. The Office located within this COMMAND-POST and its inner sanctum is the location where War was conducted on multiple scales that has only now come to light. Where the Declaration of Independence, the Bill of Rights and portions of the U.S. Constitution were drafted, and all of them in their construction, were nothing short of the waging of Wars.

Why is all of this important and how was any of this even possible? - All of this will be explained and answered within this document as we move forward.

At this particular point in time, :FEDERAL-POSTAL-JUDGE, POSTMASTER-GENERAL :Russell-Jay: Gould, was – as he still is to this very day, 24 NOVEMBER 2016 – THE LEGAL and LAWFUL, FEDERAL-POSTAL-AUTHORIZATION-CONTRACT-DOCUMENT-PROVIDER for the UNITED STATES of America - (just as the king of Great Britain once was) – and provides this Nation with all of the Global Authorizations necessary to conduct Commerce [Shipping and Trading, i.e. Business] with the rest of the Planet.

This is made possible due to the INCONTESTABLE FACT that :FEDERAL-POSTAL-JUDGE, POSTMASTER-GENERAL, COMMANDER-AND-CHIEF :Russell-Jay :Gould, with the assistance of :FEDERAL-POSTAL-JUDGE :David-Wynn: Miller, had long since established their own Sovereign Global Government System and were vested with all the Authorizations of Nation Status, by the United Nations.

Whereby it is duly recognized as well, by the VATICAN and the PENTAGON, that :COMMANDER :Gould - (before he became POSTMASTER-GENERAL in Washington DC) – the "LAND" of his country here in this world – is legally recognized as, THE LAND OF THE COURT DURING THE TIME OF CONTRACT. (Because the Contract-Document itself, is the "LAND" of the Court)

ON TOP OF THAT – He turns around and as the first order of business as the new FEDERAL-POSTMASTER-GENERAL for the Office of the Post in the Federal District of Columbia, now that his native nation is out of a state of bankruptcy, and for the first time since the Original Post Office of his nation in Philadelphia Pennsylvania, was closed down, he CORRECTLY order's the ORIGINAL-POSTAL-NATIVITY-CONTRACT-LOCATION of the Original Benjamin Franklin Post Office open and CORRECTLY legs-in as the new CORRECT SUCCESSOR to the ORIGINAL-POSTMASTER-GENERAL :Benjamin-Franklin. AND WITH THAT, he CORRECTLY becomes the NEW :POSTMASTER-GENERAL for the ORIGINAL-POST-OFFICE of the united States of America. AND AS A SOVEREIGN RULER of his own Global Government System, by his own right, is the first person in the world to ever grant this once Private Charter and Corporate Nativity Location (nation of his birth) ACTUAL SOVEREIGN NATION STATUS AND NATIONAL GLOBAL STANDING as A SOVEREIGN INDEPENDENT NATION STATE. - And all of it, for the Land of the Free and the Home of the Brave..

FINALLY, what makes this one American so special and so powerful, is the fact that with the advent and creation of his Global Government System HE TOOK DOWN and CAPTURED the entire 8,500 year old Global System of Government, known as the "Empire of the 3 City States".

Ultimately created by the "tribe of DAN"; who are themselves the inbred and autistic line of the European Lucifarian worshiping incestuous – self proclaimed - "Royal" Families from hell. Whom in association with their despotic Cousins in the Vatican - (the strong-arm of which is the Military JESUIT Militia and by extension, the Knights of Malta and the Royal Order of the Garter) - to include the Free Masons, the (now taken over) Knights Templar, the Knights of

Columbus, and the Shriners form the largest clandestine global intelligence community in the world and whom have infiltrated every aspect of Civil Authority from the ground up in their overall effort and Military Objective to pave the way for THEIR NEW WORLD ORDER.

THE TRIBE OF DAN
&
THE EMPIRE OF THE 3 CITY STATES

This information is extremely important and you need to know it in order to understand how the United States has been used, and furthermore how it has been set up to be slaughtered, and by whom.

~6. You must come to understand that the king of GB was beyond furious to learn of what had just conspired behind his back, that not only stopped his takeover of a nation that he had just spent 300 years working to conquer, but what ultimately took every last vestige of his power and authority away from him and "THE EMPIRE OF THE 3 CITY STATES", all together. [the 3 unclean spirits; Rev. KJV – Greed, Power & Control]

To include disqualifying and CAPTURING the Matriarchy and the Patriarchy on this planet. Thereby destroying the "Royal" standing of every last bloodline member of the entire Inbred Royal Family themselves [tribe of Dan] and more importantly the soul cooking, lucifarian worshiping, over-controlling, power hungry, GODLESS and SOULLESS DESPOTS residing within the confines of the "City State of the Vatican", ... and placed it all,.. every last bit of it,… right back into the hands of Almighty GOD and freed the people of the world from their Tyrannical NWO Agenda.

~7. What is "THE EMPIRE OF THE 3 CITY STATES"? The Empire of the 3 City States consists of, THE CITY OF LONDON, [representing: Greed $$] - THE (US) CITY/DISTRICT OF COLUMBIA, [representing: Power] – VATICAN CITY, [representing: Control]. - These are the 3 UNCLEAN SPIRITS in the world spoken of in the Book of Revelations. Greed, Power and Control.

~8. Who created and are in control of the 3 City States? – None other than, the tribe of Dan. * BIBLICAL GENEALOGY vs. FACTUAL HISTORICAL FAMILY BLOOD-LINE CONNECTIONS

~9. Who, or what, is the "Tribe of Dan"? - Dan was Jacob's fifth son. "Dan" means, Judge. His mother was Bilhah, a maidservant to Rachel, another one of Jacobs wives. (Genesis records his [Dan] birth as 1737 B.C.) - "Dan shall be a Serpent by the way." (Genesis; 49, 17) – Jacob speaking of his son Dan; A serpent leaves a trail, and so has the children of Dan, everywhere they went they named places, Gods, Goddesses, Tribes and every manner of thing after their Patriarch. The land they were originally given was in the North of Galilee, which gave birth to the tribe of Dan, being a sea faring people. And it is thanks to the sea faring Danes, that many of the tribes of Israel settled in foreign lands. The bulk of the Danes settled in the North of Israel, at the foot of Mount Hermon.

~10. Interestingly, Mt Hermon and the surrounding area is compared to, in the Bible, as a Unicorn. Unicorn = Tribe of Dan, = Israel & somehow,.. this tribe has connected itself to the Royal line of King David and the THRONE of JESUS CHRIST. Christ, who was the WORD OF GOD Himself made manifest in the flesh and lived, gave, loved and was sacrificed as an innocent servant to the world and as a divine ransom exchanged for the redemption of the souls of Man.

~11. Through this Mythical blood-tie the British Royals somehow covertly infer to their connection to the Biblical King David and Israel. According to Manly P. Hall's "The Secret Teachings of all ages", the serpent has always been associated with wisdom and salvation. However, it is written that the fallen angels had once again mated with the daughters of man [after the flood] and the children of the fallen angels were referred to as "the seed of the serpent", and that it is through mating with them, that the tribe of Dan are said to carry the SERPENT SEED.

~12. Two symbols that always represent both the tribe of Dan and Satan are the serpent and the dragon.

~13. Prophecy clearly states that both the CHRIST [Jesus] and the ANTICHRIST [Lucifer – rejector of GODS Laws] will both have an Earthly father from the tribe of Dan and a mother from the tribe of Judah. But the tribe of Dan has always used a serpent [snake/dragon/cobra] and interestingly enough, the Eagle in certain ways, to identify and separate their tribe from all of the other tribes of the world.

~14. The Lion (Sun=God) is commonly known as the tribe of Judah and Queen Elizabeth's Coat of Arms has 9 Lions on it and also represents Southern Israel & now England. Further, the Queen insists that she can trace her bloodline back to King David and CHRIST.

~15. The Unicorn (Moon=Goddess) Represents Northern Israel & now Scotland, of which Prince William somehow represents.

SIDE-NOTE: Of great interest is the Rothschild's Coat of Arms. This needs to be seen and compared to all of the other Coat's of Arms as it puts them all to shame. Very interesting, indeed.

~16. Very notably, Samson of the Bible, is the most famous character from the tribe of Dan and this narrative must be mentioned. - The Biblical Story states that his parents were unable to conceive, yet an angel appeared and told them they would have a son that would deliver Israel from its enemies. Their instructions were to never cut his hair and never give him alcohol. As a young adult, Samson chooses a Philistine bride and on the way to ask her hand, he is attacked by a Lion, which he rips apart, and kills. Later when he passes the dead Lion on the way to his wedding, its carcase is full of BEE'S & sweet honey of which, he takes to his wedding.

~17. Many Jews are expecting a messiah of the same lineage as Samson to return to reign triumphantly. [tribe of Dan] On the flip side many Jews also expect the ANTICHRIST to be of the same line because as foretold he will destroy the tribe of Judah [the Lion], as in the Samson story. Surprisingly, Prince William descends from the Merovingians on his mother Diana's side. They use the BEE Motive on their Crest and believe that the secret of their power lay in their long hair.

~18. Why is all of this important? It's important because a peddler of disinformation named Herbert Armstrong, a British Israelite who has written a book called "the United States of Britain" tried to pass off as fact that, the prophet Jeremiah landed in Ireland in 569 B.C. with the daughter of King Zedekiah, the last King of Judah, after being ousted by the Babylonians. He claims that the Princesses name is TEA-TEPHI and she married an Irish Prince, (WHAT PRINCE, PRINCE OF WHAT?) thereby introducing the Royal Bloodline of king David into Ireland, Scotland and then eventually England!? (WHAT PRINCE?)

~19. The fiction/fraudulent end of this account is that, Herbert Armstrong, the British Israelite that claims to have pulled this information out of the historical annuls of Irish history, is a liar. AS NONE OF IT, is to be found ANYWHERE within the annuls of any recorded Irish history.

~20. What I want you to recognize is that the overall objective of this entire story is to fool the foolish into thinking that Prince William is somehow the legitimate heir to the title of MESSIAH, and KING of.. whoever.. hailing from the divine line of King David and none of it could be further from the truth. Its all been fabricated by a group of overly inbred psychopaths that are clearly identified as an evil and CURSED TRIBE of people, by GOD Himself.

~21. This is who the entire Royal Family is and this is who they all are and what they endeavor to do. They are the drunken inbred descendants of the insidious tribe of Dan that have been working incessantly for generations to create a New World Order. (NWO)

~22. Hand in hand with the Vatican (Papal Bulls) and the Rothschild's this "TRIBE" work to wage wars, depopulate, and enslave the people to the debt of those wars. King Louie XIV of France actually called himself the SUN KING and declared that kings were born of divine [invisible] origin. Merovee was the Patriarch of the Merovingians Dynasty; he claimed to be of the bloodline of Poseidon. (Son of Apollo) He said that his mother had been raped by the sea monster. Yet, when Christianity swept through Europe, the Merovingians changed the descent of their linage, and decided instead that they were from the bloodline of King David. Louis claimed to be descendant from every god.

~23. Finally, they openly state that they are the bloodline descendants of the Annunnaki Alien visitor named Enlil, brother of Enki and son of Ea, the king of another world and off-world humanoid/lizard/serpent/dragon like, [reptilian] species, that claim to be responsible for actually engineering "Man" here on this rock by mixing their genes with a "Bigfoot" type creature to create Cro-Magnon Man. Fostering his intellectual and physical evolution to a point that eventually dovetails into the progenitors coming to breed with the Female Gender of this cross-engineered DNA spliced creation, where with the actual gestation of this inception gives birth to a true half-breed child of the two species. [Homosapien Man] This is supposedly where "kingship" originates here on this rock. It is the tie to an "off-world" throne for those children.

~24. Backtracking the family name is the easiest way to associate or validate anyone's bloodline heritage or ethnicity. When we do this, we find that the so called "Royal Family" who triumphed, is basically, German. They are seated on almost every throne, in Europe. "THEY" are, the Saxe-Co berg-Gother-Battonburg Bloodline, which often intermarries with the Hess-Castle German Nobility, and claim JEWISH DESCENT, from the Royal House of David in ancient Israel. They raise their children up, without love or compassion. Breeding each successive generation to be at the head of the Military Establishment, who keep an angered peace, BY USE OF FEAR, SURVEILLANCE and WAR.

~25. Queen Victoria was sorely hated by everyone, hissed in public, and 7 attempts on her life were made. She was a slave-driver and a tyrant, as were her relatives. Both of Prince Phillips sisters married high ranking German Officers in the German Party. His sister Sophie married S.S. Colonel Christoph Von Hess, Chief of Herman Gorings Secret Intelligence. Prince Phillips German Uncle, Lord Lewis Von Batton was a central figure in secret communications between the British Royal Family and their pro Hitler Cousins in Germany. Its a recorded fact that uncle Lewis had the nickname Dickie, because it is well known, as he was well known, to be a homosexual pedophile; as was his other Uncle George, who harbors a personal, private child pornography photo collection at Buckingham/Windsor Palace. Uncle Dickie was also found guilty of co-operating a child prostitution ring in Ireland from out of a boys care home until 1981 where he used little boys in ritual sex acts and they were sold like prostitutes to other Royals, Politicians, Layers & Judges who were never convicted of these crimes. 27 AUG 79, Uncle Dickie died when he was successfully assassinated by a bomb on his boat. Needless to say, many of the "Royals" are hopelessly mentally retarded due to the shallow gene-pool. Locked away, and forgotten, in "homes". FACT. The rest are a STRAIGHT-JACKET WORTHY CRIMINAL ORGANIZATION who live out their entire lives waging WAR on every other last living human soul on this planet in an overall effort to enslave them.

~26. These inbred, blood thirsty, power hungry, pedophiles and Lucifarian Demon worshiping murderers, are the tribe of Dan, to include every member of the VATICAN and the Jesuit Order – which is the Private Military/Melita of the Vatican. The same tribe of Dan that became the VIKINGS and in 1016 AD, the Viking king, Kanuet seized the throne of England. Since that time they have been incessantly planning to DEPOPULATE this entire planet by KILLING EVERYONE that does not share their bloodline ties. FACT.

~27. To secure these wicked ends, the EMPIRE OF THE 3 CITY STATES was constructed to create mass amounts of invisible/fiction wealth and power that could ULTIMATELY be used, to psychologically induce a trance-like condition-of-state in the mind of the individual. Where through the acceptance and use of a system that places a value of worth on a physical effort or object of some interest or desire where the overall outcome in the design of this system being to subversively swindle the people of the world with this trickery out of the realization of their GOD Given right to live and exist freely anywhere on this rock as intended by God is traded away. Ultimately enslaving not only their minds to this system but trading the physical worth of their bodies and ultimately the ground of the Earth itself they require to live upon, in for a predetermined value that was nefariously set to achieve this wicked outcome. As they would – in their final resolve – CLAIM TO OWN THE WHOLE WORLD ITSELF and EVERYTHING IN IT, and by the conformity of your acceptance of this system, to rid your useless presence upon the land, they are LITERALLY PLANNING TO KILL EVERYONE ON IT.

HISTORICAL CAVEAT:

THE SECRET SHADOW GOVERNMENT

OPENING CAVEAT:

In the global order and worldly affairs of men, it is incumbent upon us to take care to articulate - with great care – the historical occurrences of the Papacy that have taken place - in order to outline for our children - the overall long range plan of penetration designed by this global syndicate, to conquer the world and make subjects of all those who are upon it.

IN the Dark Ages, and in the power of the Popes at the time over the political government; the Kings and Queens of the Earth, as well as the Far East and then, the ensuing reformation, (the Protestant Reformation) - beginning 1517 when Luther mailed his 95 page thesis to, All Saints Church in Witenberg - and then the "counter reformation" (Declaration of war against Christianity by the Vatican), started by the Papacy and Loyola,... It's in this stream, and twisted flow of

55

medieval history that we can better understand the ASSUMED power, and FRADULENT self-serving global purpose, of the Papacy; the establishment of the Jesuit Order. HOW the Vatican was formed, WHY it was formed, and ultimately, its power and position in the world today. And also further articulate and expose all those individuals who have aligned themselves – either with, or without the knowledge, of the overall plan – with this "New World Order" and their global conspiracy to conquer and control the entire world and every living thing on it.

ASSUMED or PRETENDED POWER

(Historical account by, Eric Jon Phelps; world authority on the Vatican)

TO BEGIN WITH:

We will start with, the Dark Ages. -

There are two Popes that we wish to remember at the meridian of papal power; that these Popes exercised a power that was ABSOLUTE, it was unfettered, and we STILL CURRENTLY stand in astonishment at what they FRAUDULENTLY CLAIM TO BE. (It's all make believe, and we are all "pretending", that they have any power over anyone, or anything. It's all a game.)

The first Pope is Hildebrand; who came to power in 1073. The second Pope is innocent the 3 rd , who came to power a couple of centuries later. He was the reigning Pope in 1215. At the time he condemned the Magna Carta in England that began to be the real charter of rights for English Freemen.

NOW – In, **"Dowling's History of Romanism"** (pages: - 240) – Concerning this Pope, called Hildebrand, or later Gregory the 7 th..

Quote: - "Hildebrand was a man of uncommon genius whose ambition in forming the most arduous projects was equaled by

56

his dexterity in bringing them into execution. **Seditious, crafty and intrepid, nothing could escape his penetration, defeat his stratagem, or daunt his courage.** Haughty and arrogant beyond ALL MEASURE, obstinate, impetuous and intractable,... He looked up to the summit of universal empire, – REPEAT! - UNIVERSAL EMPIRE, with a wishful eye, and labored up the seep assent with uninterrupted ardor. An invincible perseverance, void of all principle, and destitute of every pious and virtuous feeling, he suffered little restraint in his audacious pursuits for the dictates of religion or the remonstrance's of conscious; such was the character of Hildebrand,... and his conduct was in every way suitable to it."

For no sooner did he find himself in the Papal Chair, that he displayed to the world, the most odious marks of his tyrannic ambition. Not contented to enlarge the jurisdiction to augment the opulence of the Sea of Rome, he labored indefatigably to render the Universal Church subject to the despotic government and the arbitrary power of the Pontiff alone. To dissolve the jurisdiction which Kings and Emperors have hitherto exercised over the various orders of the clergy and to exclude them from all part of management or distribution of the revenues of the church. (FACT)

Na, this outrageous Pontiff went still farther, **and impiously attempted to submit to his jurisdiction, the Emperors, Kings and Princes of the Earth and to render their dominions TRIBUTARY to the Sea of Rome.** (FACT – This was the ultimate usurpation of all power on the Earth and with this usurpation of powers, would reign-in all power under the command and control of one roof, the Vatican. But this power was taken without consent or rather, it was stolen and assumed, and therefore an act war in disobedience by the clergy and captured, with the premeditated plan to commit a fraud against the entire world to gain command and control of the world and all the people on it. And it has succeeded.)

How did this all succeed? How was the power stolen?

It was usurped quite cunningly by Hildebrand wherein he told all the Kings and Queens of the Earth - (who were not happy with the current status quo and the treatment they and their kingdoms were receiving at the hands of the current Monarch) - that they were not beholden to King Henry IV, Emperor of the Holy Roman empire, (The 1 st German Reich) but Hildebrand told them that they hold their Kingdoms as a privilege of The pope.

Even after Henry IV assembled a global council of the world's most renown and foremost scholars; and after a mature deliberation concurred and concluded that Hildebrand/Gregory 7 th ,having USURPED the chair of St. Peter by INDIRECT MEANS and infected the church of GOD with many novelties and abuses, deviated from his duty to his sovereign in several scandalous attempts; the Emperor by that supreme authority, derived from his predecessors ought to divest him of his dignity and appoint himself another in his place. Here now is a Holy Roman Emperor trying to get rid of the Pope.

And the pope turned around and told Henry, you're going to be subject to me because, if you're not, I'm going to excommunicate you. The Pope then proceeded to convene a council of 150 Bishops of the associated clergy of the kingdoms together and decree through proclamation by the authority of THE 150 Bishops and invoking the right of Almighty God - (that he had no authority to do) - that all of the Roman Catholic peoples of the kingdoms therein were to no longer recognize Henry as The Holy Roman Emperor. This was a massive act of war.

This is the most classic act of a war that we, as GOD Fearing Americans and free men, must all know and remember as, THE MOST POWERFUL MOMENT IN THE HISTORY OF WARFARE IN THE WORLD. This was the greatest war ever to take place over the temporal powers on planet Earth, ever recorded. (Until 2 NOV 1999 when the United States came out of its 3 rd and final, international bankruptcy - See :David-Wynn: Miller, :Russell-Jay: Gould, and QUANTUM LANGUAGE)

So with the audacity and cunning morose ambition, of which the likes of have never been seen, under the threat of excommunication by the Pope, as all the Monarchs of the world were in disapproval of the current status quo, and who sought to remove some of King Henry's infringements, once deceived by the Pope in his attempt to capture all of these powers - (as they didn't see it coming as such) - gave up all rights and powers of their kingdoms to the Pope in fear of being excommunicated AND CURSED by the Pope, and DE-NOUNCED as KINGS or QUEENS. Wherein the Pope used a ruse and/or trickery to attack the Kings and Queens, and in an act of disobedience and war, would prepare a proclamation, or an edict by the church - (where he had no right or power) - nor did he truly have jurisdiction to do so, and proceeded to denounce the Monarchy's position, and disavow and curse their crowns. (It was a massive gamble by the Pope.)

So out of the fear of being excommunicated and cursed, rather than just sacking the Pope and arresting him as a conspirator and traitor to the crown and freedoms of the world that he was, these Kings and Queens, all bowed down to the Pope and surrendered their Kingdoms to him without so much as one single military struggle. This cunning move was how Hildebrand used the weakness of support in the current Monarch to his advantage and devised a divide and conquer tactic, ultimately coupled with FEAR, to usurp the power of every kingdom on planet Earth, and bring them all under his eternal reign. And at the time, he did it void of an Army of his own.

Today, in the 21 st Century, he has the Jesuit Militia. Which is his very own PRIVATE MILITIA; and they openly state that they are NOT a religious organization to everyone on the planet, and they are in FACT, the Militia for the Vatican. Ultimately if any King/Ruler fails to yield their obedience to the church, they can expect to be excommunicated and dethroned. - THIS HOLDS VERY TRUE TODAY! -

(This is a classic example of the Papacy exercising its Temporal Powers) How many Jesuit Schools are in your town?

CAVEAT: -

a.) (We see that Hildebrand was extremely DRIVEN and exceptionally intelligent, we must attribute this to almost every Pope thereafter. These men are extremely focused intellectual geniuses. They have visions and dreams of fulfilling what they desire; which is: UNIVERSAL SPIRITUAL POWER and UNIVERSAL TOMPORAL POWER.) [Absolute power over the spirit and the flesh, on all of the Earth]

b.) (We must not forget that in 606, the Pope was given [assumed] Universal Spiritual Power and 150 years later in 756, he was given [assumed] Universal Temporal Power. Every Pope thereafter sought to enlarge and enhance these two assumed powers.)

c.) (These two assumed powers are represented on the Papal Flag flying in front of any Catholic School – OR, in my nearby area, a Jesuit [Vatican Militia] School – one of the flags they fly is the Papal Flag, which is a Crown of the Pope - a triple crown with two keys crossed - each key symbolizing the powers of the Pope. The first is the Universal Spiritual Power; where every creature is to be subject to the spiritual power of the Pope. And the other key is his Universal Temporal Power... and every King and every military dictator and every president and every prime minister is to be subject to his rule. - It is these two powers that the Papacy works - WITH ALL OF THEIR MIGHT DAY AND NIGHT – in a conspiracy against all the governments of man, to establish making the "White Pope" (the visible front man dressed in white) the UNIVERSAL MONARCH OF THE WORLD.)

d.) (This is the foundation, this is the THEOLOGICAL FOUNDATION, for what we call today... THE NEW WORLD ORDER.) -

The New World Order is NOTHING MORE, than a reversion back to the "Old World Order" - which was the dark ages of the Papacy, or what is also referred to as the "Iron Age of Man".

CONTINUING:

In Dowling's "History of Romanism", pg. 240, we read –

QUOTE - "The views of Hildebrand, or Hell-brand, as from his insane ambition, as he has been appropriately styled, were not confined to the erection of an absolute Universal MONARCHY in the Church,... they aimed also at the establishment of a CIVIL MONARCHY, equally as extensive and despotic. And this aspiring Pontiff, after having drawn up a system of ecclesiastical cannons, (cannons being MAN MADE laws, Codes or Statues) for the government of the church, would have introduced a new code of political laws, had he been permitted to execute the plan he had formed."

This is what is happening, RIGHT NOW, in The United States of America as these very Codices & Statutes and this entire ancient plan – (long ago shelved and set aside for this very moment in time) - are finally - (after long wait by the Vatican) - rolled out and shoved down our throats, disguised as the maxim's of Corporate mandates adopted drunkenly as the International Codes & Statutes of Admiralty and Maritime Law of the Sea the masquerading as Public Justice Policies.

His purpose was (as stated and outlined by Mosheim, the PREMIER Protestant Historian, in his work, the book: "The History of the Church").

QUOTE: - "To engage in the bonds of fidelity an allegiance to St. Peter, i.e. to The Roman Pontiffs, all the Kings and Princes of the Earth, and to establish in Rome (The United Nations?) an annual assembly of Bishops, by whom the contests that might arise amongst and between kingdoms of sovereign states, were to be decided. The rights and pretensions of Princes would be examined and the FATE OF NATIONS and EMPIRES, TO BE DETERMINED."

Making this – IN SIMPLE LANGUAGE – the Pope, or "Hell-brand" CLAIMED,... that he had the RIGHT,... to a UNIVERSAL MONARCHY IN THE EARTH and was TO BE THE KING OF THE WORLD AND EVERYONE ON IT. That he was the one to establish that Monarchy and that any problems between Monarchs in their various kingdoms or sovereign states, WERE TO BE DECIDED BY HIMSELF. (OR THE PAPACY)

Do you now understand why the Pope has an honorary chair at the United Nations?

It is here, that HE INSISTS HE HAS THE RIGHT, to decide the FATE OF NATIONS. The future of wars, how the cold war will be waged and while always, UNDER THE GUISE OF CALLING FOR PEACE. But in fact, he is the mover and shaker of EVERY WAR, at least since the beginning of the Counter Reformation. (A Declaration of War on the Protestant Movement of the open worship of Jesus Christ, aka. the Take-Down, of The United States) in 1540 with Ignacius Loyola's establishment of the Jesuit Order. (VATICAN MILITIA/ARMY) - Whose job it is to infiltrate, manipulate, and subdue all aspects of every government on Earth, and report back to the Pope; work to create laws and legislation that will undermine Free Governments, eradicate Nationalism, and further the ONE WORLD GOVERNMENT AGENDA UNDER THE DICTATES OF THE GLOBAL MONARCHY.)

So here we have the most notorious individual – (not just a self-proclaimed Global MONARCH, but the most notorious Human Being to ever walk the planet) – Hildebrand, swatting the Kings and Queens of the Earth under threat, and the duress he's created, with these PRETENDED "powers" that he ASSUMINGLY "CLAIMS" that he has the right to wield, self-authorizes the usurpation and illegal, fraudulent sequestration of those all-encompassing global monarchical powers. All the while, still walking around as though what he did he shouldn't be ashamed of; not in the eyes of GOD or Christ, for what it is that he has done, nor for what it is that the Papacy will continue to do from that point. This is their Legacy.

As it has been plainly laid out by the Vatican itself, the Pope does not believe in any separation of Church and State and wholly denounces any such belief or practice in any system of government to the contrary. All power of government throughout the known world rests under the roof of the Vatican and – (according to this small group of old men) – is directly within their sole circumspection to exercise it against anyone they see fit. The Vatican is against any form, or system of government, that grants sovereign rights to any individual; as all rights and freedoms are a grant, or conferred, - (only according to these old men) - through the power of the Papacy alone. Which are nothing more the dictates of another mans conscience, over ones own. (Spiritual, mental and physical, SLAVERY.)

In the eyes of the Papacy it is Not the free will of man granted by GOD, bestowed through divine decree, - ("do what thou wilt, shall be the whole of the law") - that gives/grants and blesses man with the freedom in life and divine authority to live it as he sees fit for himself. NO; In the eyes of the Papacy, NO MAN has any sovereign free will of any kind here in this 3-dimensional reality, unless the Papacy says so. (Placing himself over GOD and all other men, tyrannically violating every-mans GOD given free will, subjugating all as his servants, subjects, and slaves.)

The Vatican is against true political power that would give any kind of liberty to a nation's subjects – (specifically in England) – and the Pope is against any divesting of his spiritual power to any other Kings, Priests or Bishops. The Vatican has endeavored tirelessly and consolidated everything into his hands. All of this has been done to control and operate in the highest level of imagined – OR PRETENDED – psychological warfare possible, by sadistically and psychopathically manipulating the superstitious minds of the people in the world around them, in an effort to make them WORSHIP THE POPE, - (Simply nothing more himself, than an ordinary old man) - as GOD on Earth. This is delusional insanity.

This whole pretended game is ludicrous and full grown men only participate and play along because they themselves are caught up in the usury of the current monetary system that we have all enslaved ourselves to,... or they do it out of their own blinded, self-serving ambition. None the less, they then put on their little work/play costume and are paid (with something) in return for "PRETENDING" that the costume gives them power to mindlessly subjugate all of the other free people of the world around them; and it's all done at the behest of just another man. These costume wearing men are nothing more than trained dogs, playing the game of a bunch of old men.

This is nothing more than a game, contrived long ago by lunatics attempting to actually claim that they are the owners, or have now – (through an imaginary system/game of pretended commerce) – seized ownership of the natural resources of the world, and with that, the world itself. A game of world asset (natural resources) backed credit, that this entire invisible system of commerce was created and based on to begin with long ago, in this meticulously thought out and diabolically executed plan,... With the end result being, the psychological manipulation of everyone into thinking, and even agreeing to, and going along with, the PRETENDED and IMAGINARY THOUGHT, that this group of old men, now actually own the whole world itself, and all of the people on it. And all of it, in all of its fraudulent imaginary authorization is being carried out to swindle every nation on Earth out of the lodial and title of the nations actual physical assets - (being the very ground beneath their feet) – and are unwittingly being militarily forced to then hand it all over to the despotic, command and control, of the Bank/Vatican and the Papacy.

The vehicle used to carry out this Frey is the system of FRACTUALIZED BANKING, in conjunction with the greed driven imaginative invention of COMPENSITORY INTEREST; monies to be paid in excess – (and even at reoccurring time driven expectational intervals) - wherein over time, and cumulatively as a nation of people, the interest paid back were exceedingly far beyond that of what was originally borrowed. And when you defaulted, the Bank/Vatican, instead of confiscating and selling the goods and possessions that were bought using that currency, whatever was borrowed, to include the interest, (pretend money) was demanded back by the Bank/Vatican, in HARD NATIONAL ASSETS; the nations HARD national resources that the fake money (credit) was all backed by, and created from in the first place. The lands of every nation on Earth are continually being seized globally by the Bank/Vatican, using this diabolically contrived, criminal swindling system.

With that, the people of the world are/were swindled and/or "bamboozled" out of their nation's natural resources and their birthright inheritance. Now the people of those nations pretend that there are no more metals, rocks, or minerals to base a currency off of in their country because the Vatican "NOTIONALLY" - (in the land of make believe) - owns all of the rocks and the dirt, and even pretends that it magically owns the water, the air, and even the sky. - (Every bit of it, CRIMINALLY FRAUDULENT - from its inception and premeditated intention to achieve the end of its objectives, and in all its actions to criminally defraud the world and the people therein, with and through the use of this battle-plan, is sick, to say the least; if not downright, straight-jacket worthy, insane.)

It is literally written in the HOLY Christian BIBLE, that GOD Himself instituted Sovereign Nations. - (not the Pope) - And Sovereign Nations are to be governed by the people of that Nation according to their desires. They are NOT to be "governed" by the Papacy; by a "FOREIGN SOVEREIGN"; thereby overthrowing the Sovereignty of that country, void of any TRUE consent, from the people themselves, that constitute the existence of that sovereign nation.

A true Bible reading, GOD Fearing and believing Christian Man, is a Patriot. And all those who stand with him on the rock that constitutes this ground are also, themselves patriots. He, and therefore they, sustains their sovereign nation. They have an allegiance to their race, their language, their culture, and the geographic boundaries of their nation, and he and therefore they, will die to sustain it. THAT is a Patriot; those are Patriots and that, is Patriotism. Even the conglomeration of clergy that make up the Papacy, are themselves Patriots,... Patriots to Rome.

65

Yet, this kind of patriotism, ROME overthrows. This kind of Nationalism, ROME overthrows. And it overthrows it pursuant to CANON Law. (CANON'S are laws made by MAN; the Pope to be exact. [Man made Laws] - They are NOT, Nor do they have anything to do with the Laws of GOD found in the worlds Holy Christian Bible.)

THE PROTESTANT REFORMATION

THE Protestant Reformation, was the glorious beginning of the LORD'S "beating-down" of the Popes Temporal Power here in the real world on Earth, with the consecrated founding and Holy Christian Establishment of, The United States of America, Herself.

QUOTE: by, R. W. Thompson; SECRETARY of The American NAVY (1870's) - from the book: "Footprints of the Jesuits"; (written in 1894) -

QUOTE: "In the times before the Reformation, the temporal affairs of governments were required to conform to the CANONS of Ecclesiastical Authority; that is, the Pope. And it was HELL to be a necessary and essential part of [that] religion, "Romanism"; that this union should be continued no matter what might be the degree of popular ignorance and humiliation" -

AGAIN: The Pope does not believe in the separation of a legitimate government and the power of the church and the Papacy. There is no other sovereign government that exists autonomously anywhere in the world that is free from the tyranny of ROME and the Papacy.

HOWEVER - It is written, as spoken by Christ Himself;

John 14:6 - **"Jesus saith unto him, I am the way, the truth, and the life: no man cometh unto the Father, but by me."**

The Pope is NOT Jesus. All of the Popes "authorizations" are PRETENDED and/or "make-believe", as he cannot authorize your entrance into heaven, nor forgive you of your sins. Every little old man that has ever claimed to be a "Pope", is himself nothing more than just a little old man, who owes the salvation of his own GOD given soul, to the LORD and Savior, Jesus Christ.

As Jesus Christ was The Son of GOD, and was sacrificed as a ransom, and crucified for the sins of the world, and therefore the sins of all men - (to include the Pope's) - to redeem their souls for GOD, - (as they are now and forevermore bought and paid for by Christ's sacrifice) - the Pope and all of his pretended spiritual and temporal/physical power has been – (AND IS INFINITUM) - forevermore, dissolved and disqualified! This means that the Pope is NOTHING MORE than a man sitting up at the Vatican in a normal old wooden chair, made right here on Earth, demanding that the world, and its leaders bow down to him, kiss his ring, submit their kingdoms to him, and ask him – (rather than Christ) - for forgiveness; thereby disregarding and denouncing the Omnipotent Spiritual and Temporal Power of the ordained sacrifice of our Lord and Savior, JESUS CHRIST.

1 Timothy 2:5 - **"For there is one God, and one mediator between God and men, the man Christ Jesus;"**

With the production of the King James Bible men could come to know the word of GOD in their own language without needing it explained to them. And with that, the Cardinals and the Priests were no longer needed, and in all actuality, never really were.

The Protestant Reformation [movement] – (the movement away from the tyranny of the Roman Catholic Church) – is the sole reason, of the why and how, The United States was founded. This is the quintessential reason that this country was settled. Settled by a small group of people who were so spiritually oppressed that they left a world, and the only place they had ever known, and risked their lives to forge a new one. Either way, it was die at the hands of the mad-men of the Vatican, or die by their own right, free from the tyranny and dictates of another mans will and conscience, whomsoever.

Freedom of conscience for everyman and the freedom thereof to exercise and express it; freely and openly as it was intended to be as given by GOD to every man.

This great gift of GOD, that was given to all men by Him, is the benevolent endowment, bestowed equally unto all men, by God Himself, that will reign eternally glorified in the sovereign existence and the FREE WILL OF EACH INDIVIDUAL MAN; as man is created in the divine physical and spiritual image of God. "Do what thou wilt shall be the whole of the law." Man is God on Earth. (All Men are the Sons and Daughters of God.)

Psalm 82:6 - **"I have said, Ye are gods; and all of you are children of the most High."**

John 10:34 - **"Jesus answered them, Is it not written in your law, I said, Ye are gods?"**

John 14:12, 13 - **"Verily, verily, I say unto you, He that believeth on me, the works that I do shall he do also; and greater works than these shall he do; because I go unto my Father. Whatever you ask in My name, that will I do, so that the Father may be glorified in the Son."**

No man needs to ask another man, especially some old man calling himself, "A Pope", for the forgiveness of Heaven, or for "permission" to do anything here is this world.

John 14: 13 - **"Whatever you ask in My name, that will I do, so that the Father may be glorified in the Son."**

Before the King James Version of The Holy Bible of GOD was released for all men to read, so that they could come to know GOD for themselves, the VATICAN and the Tyranny of the Roman Catholic Church, with the Pope as its head, would hunt men and women down for practicing any religion outside of the Roman Catholic Church. Wherein once these people were found they were burned at the stake alive. In most instances, these people were taken in the middle of the night from their homes, under the cover of darkness and against their unsuspecting free will by the most cowardly of men, and tortured at great lengths into false confessions, before they were murdered in the inhumane and UNGODLY manor that they were, in the name of the Vatican.

(All men are created in the image of GOD, therefore to kill any man, is to kill GOD.) -

Such was the daily, and/or nightly, work of the - (I dare not call them men) - individuals of the Vatican and the Roman Catholic Church. Please understand, this was a real and regular occurrence as a practice of the Vatican; and if they ever gain the global control, to rule the way that they want... That very same activity will once again ensue, only this time, FULL THROTTLE. (This is written)

The entire religious dogma of the Roman Catholic Church is an unholy fabrication invented and designed for the purposes of creating wealth and controlling entire regions of human beings.

However, The Scottish Rites, on the other hand, are not recognized as any part of the Roman Catholic Church, nor associated with any of its fundamental orthodox practices. Yet, The Scottish Rites and the ritualistic magical rites thereof are very well recognized and very much practiced and invoked with great ceremony by the entire congregation of the Papacy. These are also known as the magical rites of King Solomon, who himself, was a master of these sacred rites, and what is referred to as, a master of divinity. As in their practice, these ritualistic magical rites were also known as invoking the rites of divinity and/or practicing, or the practice of, divination; the practice of being divine, and/or Godlike. As in his creation and existence, it is divinely recognized that man is created in the immortal image of GOD Himself and therefore, in the opulence and divine presence of his holy physical manifestation in this 3-dimensional kingdom, is given all authority in Heaven itself too, through the secret knowledge contained therein, exercise and practice these rites as a matter of his own sovereign right of conscience, and consecrated inheritance of absolute Holy free will.

These divine practices were not to be taken lightly and with their understanding came a great deal of responsibility. As these magical rites and the secrets of what could be obtained in their use were understood, they were kept highly guarded and their use was eventually relegated to the right of Kings alone; this however also included the men of the Clergy and the Roman Catholic Church. Those outside of those chosen realms caught practicing these rituals or rites, were put to death for witch-craft and/or charged, in the name of GOD, with heresy against the church, as the men who now controlled these powerful practices were afraid that it would be found and realized that this practice was the divine rite of all men, as each is created in the image of Almighty God, Himself.

These are the men associated with the Vatican and the tyrannical works of divinity revolving around the Roman Catholic Church and the spiritual and temporal oppressive mysticism and sorcery, thereof; this, and of course much more, were the reasons that the men of this day and age were living in fear and searching for any place in the world that would provide them with rest, if even only for a short while, from the unrelenting tyrannies and abuses of this government and its self-declared monarch.

The United States of America is considered the Body of Christ, and as the Body of Christ, the foundation for our system of Government is based on His Statues; **Take care of the Tired, the Poor, the Sick and the Hungry; not to forget the Widowed and/or the Orphaned.** These systems are a direct foundational reflection of Christianity in this Nation, His Church, and therefore His Body; the Body of The United States; the body of Jesus Christ. If the Vatican is ever going to rule over GODS People, the Body of Christ must first be laid to rest. And it all started as soon as they had the opportunity, with the removal of prayer from our Schools. (If the Vatican had anything to do with the work of Christ, or GOD, prayer would have never been removed from this nations educational program.)

The command circle of the Royal Order of the Vatican Militia, ran by the Jesuit General of the Vatican Militia, is known as, The **Order of the Knights of Saint John of Jerusalem**; yet it has NOTHING to do with Jesus Christ or the works around the world thereof. The Lieutenants of that Order are called the Knights of Malta and they are all LITERALLY men who have been Royally Knighted and hold Royal Knighthoods in this global, new world order. Sir Henry Kissinger is the HIGHEST RANKING Knight of Malta, for the order and works as a Lieutenant for the Committee of 300. That is a matter of public record, and an indisputable fact. -

The Founding Fathers of The United States very well knew this and very well understood who their enemies were, as did J.F. Kennedy. This is the reason The Declaration of Independence and The U.S. Constitution were drafted, and outline specifically what the role of Government is. It is a SERVANT to the people, NOT ITS MASTER. The United States is a government, "OF THE PEOPLE, BY THE PEOPLE, AND FOR THE PEOPLE." UNLIKE the case with the Papacy and the Roman Catholic Church with the Pope as its Head of State, and self-proclaimed omnipotent Global Monarch.

Which the ultimate resolve of this Monarch has been to infiltrate the government of the United States and work to tear down and destroy the Sovereign Declaration of ONE NATION UNDER GOD, outside of the monotheistic rule of the Papacy and the tyranny of the Roman Catholic Church and its vision of a Monarchical NEW WORLD ORDER; AGAIN... with the Pope as its Global Head of State.

: HENCE; The U.S. Constitution - 2nd AMENDMENT - "The right of the Citizens to keep and bear Arms, SHALL NOT BE IN-FRINGED." -

---

IGNATIUS LOYOLA
THE COUNTER REFORMATION
and
THE JESUIT ORDER aka. THE VATICAN MILITIA

1). The Counter Reformation is a declaration of war against the Protestant Doctrine of Christianity and by extension The United States of America Herself, The Ten Commandments of GOD, and the Gospel Truths and pure Doctrines of our Lord and Savior, Jesus Christ.

2). This declaration of war is being initiated at the Vatican by private decree of the Papacy and is designed to destroy the Laws of GOD that the United States was founded upon through acts of international espionage and terrorism of the highest order to further advance its religious warfare efforts to remove the Church of Jesus Christ and His Doctrines from the face of the Earth and replace them with the MAN MADE CANON LAWS of The Vatican.

3). The overall objective of this battle-plan is to destroy the Declaration of Independence and The U.S. Constitution whereby the foundation of The United States will collapse in conjunction with an orchestrated systematic take-down of the removal and banishment of The Ten Commandments and the Laws of Almighty GOD that provided and constitute the very cornerstone from which all systems of State and Federal Government were promulgated upon with the HOLY Establishment and Consecrated Founding of The United States of America.

4). The final objective(s) of this declaration of war is to subdue all the governments of man on Earth and bring them under the totalitarian spiritual and temporal "command and control" of the Vatican and the Papacy; to genocide the practice and/or knowledge of all religions repugnant to the Roman Catholic Church from the face of the Earth; to ultimately capture and seize command and control of the City of Jerusalem from the Muslims in Israel, and once again rebuild and reconstitute The Temple Mount at The Dome of the Rock, where – once inside - a man will draw his own blood using "The Spear of Destiny" and declare that he is "god on Earth", and force the other men on this planet [Rock] to worship him as such, or be murdered.

This battle plan and its associated objectives are to be executed and carried out by the Knights of Malta and by extension, the Jesuit Militia of the Vatican; which is also the largest clandestine intelligence network on the planet. This network moves with absolute Carte Blanche, through the quite actions of its senior ranking officers (some, Knighted individuals) that have infiltrated every government and mysteriously – (yet blatantly) – hold multiple command and control key positions in the top-most offices in every government globally. Offices that were set up to watch over each other respectively in a system of "checks and balances", that have now been infiltrated by the criminals, to work them in conjunction with one another to conspire, – (especially within National jurisdictions where these tactics are primarily needed and carried out) - and commit their acts of war and espionage, against any nation of peaceful people undetected; without having to answer to anyone for anything that they're doing. The end result being the take-down and destruction of the sovereignty of that nation, and the enslavement of the people themselves.

How these men are considered above the law and out of the reach of all of the other government agencies on Earth that are in place to protect their respected sovereign nations and territories, can all be answered by looking at the Vatican, and more importantly, ITS MILITIA.

The 1 st General of the Jesuit Militia, IGNATIUS LOYOLA obtained his power over the Pope and all authority on Earth the same way that Hildebrand obtained his. IGNATIUS knew that without him and his work in coordinating all of the espionage and warfare needed by the Papacy to bring the NEW WORLD ORDER into existence for Rome, the plans of the Papacy would never succeed. So he threated the Pope and told him as much. However, he conjured, if the Papacy would grant him supreme military autonomy – ABOVE EVEN THE POPE AND THEREFORE ALL POWERS ON EARTH – to enable him to conduct his works unhindered, he would give his loyalty to the Vatican to achieve these ends. The Pope at that time knew this was a massive gamble, and the Pope today knows very well, that the General of the Jesuit Militia holds a higher position of authority on Earth than even himself, as Pope.

The General of the Jesuit Militia, this man that holds a higher Military Authority than any other Military General in the World, who holds a higher position of authority on Planet Earth than even even the Pope himself,… has always been known within the realms of this Order, as the Black Pope.

The Papacy granted the 1 st General of the Jesuit Militia - (IGNATIUS LOYOLA) - absolute unbridled military autonomy and with it, global Carte Blanche – (PRESIDING EVEN OVER THAT OF THE VATICAN) - to move and act on behalf of the Vatican free from all law globally and free from all apprehension of any authority on Earth. Even when acting in violation of national and/or international laws despite any recognized law that may be being violated by the Jesuit Agents, as they work to move around the globe conducting all manner of their hell worthy and illegal, criminal activities against those sovereign nation-states in their efforts to literally work the corruption and sabotage, of those nations.

In short, this is a group of bad-guys working to destroy all the nations and governments of man on the Earth, and when the bad-guys are caught by the "good-guy" agents - (for working their criminal warfare) - they are released by those nations "good-guy" agents, without being charged for their criminal actions, whatsoever. Making them untouchable and above apprehension from any law, anywhere.

This group, now finally recognized as the criminal syndicate that it is, and the individuals that constitute its existence, need to be individually identified and arrested as the International Spy's and global saboteurs that they are, and incarcerated.

CAVEAT:

IF WE PLAY BY THEIR RULES -

(THIS IS THE ACHILLES HEEL OF THE N.O.W. If this circle can be infiltrated, the power of its autonomous supreme immunity from legal apprehensions can be used to take down the entire system, to include the arrest and incarceration of the Pope himself as a criminal mastermind. As in its grant to this supreme position, all who are vested with these authorities are free even from the CANONS and the LAWS and/or the DICTATES of the Pope because in fact and in deed, even the Pope is powerless against its position over him.

This is the greatest point of weakness in the NWO, and the Pope is very aware of it. He is aware of it because he knows that without this group of individuals doing his biddings/work and carrying out the acts of espionage and sabotage that must be conducted to bring the N.W.O. into fruition, plans of the N.W.O. will never succeed. This is why their absolute loyalty to these ends must be without question. This is where the General of the Militia stands, as the Black Pope. This also makes infiltration extremely unlikely. But if the individuals can be educated to the awareness of the fact that even their own family members will not be immune to the punishments that are yet to be meted out, - KNIGHTED INDIVIDUALS OR NOT - there would be an even earlier "falling away" from these pretended loyalty's, then prophesied.)

BUT ONLY, IF WE CONTINUE TO PLAY BY THE RULES OF THEIR GAME AND CONTINUE TO SUBMIT, AS KING HENRY IV DID, INSTEAD OF SACKING THEM, AS KING HENRY IV, SHOULD HAVE DONE.

These individuals and their works, in their EVERY ENDEAVOR, have NOTHING to do with our LORD and SAVIOR Jesus Christ and NEVER HAVE.

END HISTORICAL CEAVEAT:

CONTINUING -

~28. That is what the Empire of the 3 City States is, this is its purpose, this is who and what the "Royal Family" really are in opposition to the rest of us. They are the Monsters of the tribe of Dan, perhaps even in the literal sense more-so than once realized, and THANK GOD, this entire tribe and their system of Monarchical Feudalism has been destroyed and taken down by COMMANDER-AND-CHIEF :Russell-Jay: Gould.

Since 1999, the news of what POSTMASTER-GENERAL, FEDERAL-POSTAL-JUDGE :Russell-Jay: Gould has done, has been kept a SECRET and kept from everyone in the United States and the World at large, by the Ruling Elite.

This has been suppressed by the Royal Families [tribe of DAN] and their Federal minions due to the fact that with the close of their Federal Postal Contract Location, the authorizations and their ability to create revenue through the Internal Revenue Service (IRS) in conjunction with the Birth Certificate System in the United States of America, has now come to an end. Which is why they have incorporated Guam, Puerto Rico, and the Virgin Islands. And if you haven't heard, Puerto Rico just backed out of the union because the Birth Certificate Taxation and Enslavement System was just about to be implemented there, as well; and they said the hell with that.

Since 1999, all of the elections that have been run here in the original 50 States, have been a fraud. Along with all of the Laws, or Mandates, to especially include the ridiculous and Tyrannical Executive Orders that have not only been DICTATED down to "We the People" in an act of fraud, but are in fact, Declarations of WAR against us. Since 1999, the plan to take over and surrender the United States, has illegally proceeded forward. The kings men [Federal Government Employees] and their entire Private Foreign DEFUNCT Federal Government System is forcing its TYRANNICAL "Rule of Law" into the State's Territories using the end of the 3 rd Bankruptcy to justify their authority to step in, destroy every last vestige of American Freedom, and force their illegal, fraudulent take-over.

What is happening, is that an envoy of Agents from the Federal Department of Homeland Security (FDHS) are going into the States Territories and informing the Civil Authorities, local Police Departments, Sheriffs Departments, etc.. that, the United States is broke and has no more money. Soon the financial system will collapse and anarchy will ensue. All of the States' Civil Authorities are now being corralled [captured] into and under the umbrella of the Federal Department of Homeland Security in an effort to ensure the "Continuity of Government", and will be used further in the effort to quell civil disobedience and keep the peace, as that time arises.

The fact is, the IMF/WORLD BANK (Rothschild, the kings system) is providing the Governors of the States Territories with the money to fund the Civil Authorities because they have now been ILLEGALLY SURRENDERED and TAKEN OVER, and when everything collapses those contingencies will continue to get paid. That is because unbeknownst to those poor unaware American Souls, (Civilians on Patrol - COPS) they are working for the king of Great Britain, and have been, since they were captured by the FDHS. They will then be TRICKED and FORCED into attacking their own country and their own countrymen in a CLANDESTINE ACT OF WAR against their Brothers in Arms, to the Nations detriment. They will be ordered to seize fire-arms, ammunition, food cashes, water cashes,.. cashes of all kinds. And many will be rounded up and killed in this effort. -

This is the War-Plan that is currently being executed by the "Empire of the 3 City States" in their attempt to illegally take-over and surrender this Nation and its Flag, and further corral [capture] every other Nation into and under, the command and control of the New World Order (NWO).

Since 1999, What has been continuing to operate up in Washington DC, is nothing short of a TOTAL FRAUD. Running illegally and as a Violent Declaration of War against this entire Nation… if not the world itself.

THE RECKONING

The reason that all of this continues to Fraudulently run, in spite of all that :POSTMASTER-GENERAL, FEDERAL-POSTAL-JUDGE :Russell-Jay: Gould has done, is due to the fact that he does not have an Army at his back to substantiate his Standing nor to enforce his Authority within those Positions here in the United States as its new POSTMASTER-GENERAL. Nor is what he has done known by the Masses of the Soldiers of the U.S. Military. Nor to the masses of the general population of "We the People", here in the United States. THAT IS WHY THE ILLEGAL SURRENDER CONTINUES TO MOVE FORWARD!

The reason that the Declaration of War by the NWO has not been challenged and stopped is because, when :FEDERAL-POSTAL-JUDGE :Russell-Jay: Gould, was in the Office of the Deputy Director for the NSA, he was told by that Deputy Director, -

(EXAGGERATED VERSION, of a First-Hand Account)

"You know what Russell, you are CORRECT. You are the Guy, the American :FEDERAL-POSTAL-JUDGE, that has taken command and control of the entire world and its System for Governing the Planet, and captured it. You're the :POSTMASTER-GENERAL of the United States of America, the :COMPTROLLER OF THE GLOBAL-CURRENCY. You own and have taken control of all banking [commerce] on Planet Earth. YES, You are this guy…and we all know it. But just because you're right, doesn't give you the might… and until you have an Army at your back, or the Army of the United States actually comprehends and recognizes what it is that you have done for this Nation, to include them and their children… Good-luck exercising any of that authority. – The fact is,

78

the American people will NEVER believe you and what it is that you've done. - They won't believe you because they're TOO GOD-DAMNED STUPID TO UNDERSTAND WHAT THE HELL IT IS THAT YOU'VE EVEN DONE; and because of that, they'll never believe it. They're just too god-damned stupid. - So good luck trying to stop any of this."

This report will attempt to validate the claims behind the outline as now presented to you. This report and the effort behind it, is to get this information and the facts that support its claims in front, and into the hands of the Elite Members and the Commando's, of the US Military Special Operations Command. The desire behind this Report, is that those Elite Personnel, knowing God-Damned good and well that this is the truth of these matters. - As no one individual could make such claims and continually work under the Titles associated and attached to such Global Locations of Power and live to talk about it, unless it were true. - That those Forces will move with GOD'S Speed and descend upon that location and secure that package and his family members and move them to a safe location before they are lost to an evil in the world – that at this point in time – can still be defeated.

This is my prayer to my Brothers in the Special Operations Community, this is my prayer to GOD, and this is my prayer, as I write this report. As GOD as my witness. :Russell, is one of my best friends, and I know the history of all of this information, to be matter of many facts. -

What :COMMANDER :Russell-Jay: Gould, risk's his life to do every day, he does for you, our Country, and our Flag; and because he knows that he is CORRECT… and fact that he is correct, is the only reason that he is still alive today. What he has been graced by GOD to do, has been provided for us by GOD, through :Russell, as divine right. - What I mean by that is :Russell, did not draw a pentagram on the ground on the full-moon of the Summer Solstice and summon Demons down in a communal effort gain this knowledge and use it to rule those around him, like they do at the top of the Pyramid.

Unlike those individuals who claim to be kings and tyrannically lord over us, COMMANDER :Gould, did it to set us all free from them and their entire evil system; ...and by GOD, he has. -

:Disclaimer – The timetable(s) associated with the events that took place and are relayed within this report, are not in the actual chronicled order that they factually took place in, but are altered for the purpose of simplifying what happened, and is done in an effort to not complicate the story.

INTEGRITY

The definition of Integrity is, "To do the right thing all the time, every time, even when no-one is watching." -

In the community of the Special Operations Forces of the United States Military, we pride ourselves in the endowment of this virtue and integrate it into every aspect of our lives. This is what makes us great. This is what sets us apart and identifies us, to those like us, as Honorable Men, Men of our Word,... Proud,... and damned few.

THE UNITY-STATES OF OUR WORLD-CORPORATION
- THE TAKE-DOWN OF ALL GLOBAL POWERS -

The Correct Sentence Structure Communication Parse Syntax Grammar (C.S.S.C.P.S.G.) is the proper nomenclature used to describes/articulate the way in which letters are brought together to form words.

OPENING CAVEAT:

(What you are about read, is some of the most highly sensitive, and once classified information on planet Earth, and has directly to do

with matters of national and global security. It has been kept classified to some degree at certain levels, and only now, after 20 years
has this information been allowed to be openly released, thereby
making it PUBLIC INFORMATION, and clear of any military, or
State Department related restrictions and/or, classifications.) -

ON THE DAY OF: 6 APRIL 1988, the mathematical interface between math and grammar was broken by, FEDERAL-POSTAL-
JUDGE: David-Wynn: Miller and FEDERAL-POSTAL-JUDGE:
Russell-Jay: Gould, wherein, it was demonstrated and proven, that
all languages can be expressed in a mathematical
equation of Algebra. $1+2=3/3-2=1$.

OFFICE of the POST MASTER GENERAL

The fact of the matter is that we are all on time-tables here on this
planet. Time-tables that run on 7 year national and 70 year international bankruptcies. These bankruptcies have controlled the planet
for the last 6,500 years in all countries. All countries world-wide are
controlled by the Post-Office; NOT the Courts, NOT the Judges,
NOT the Kings and Queens, but the Post-Masters of the world run
the entire planet and have for 6,700 years; going all the way back to
Pharaoh (Hence, the Masons).

And whose Calendar do all of the governments on planet Earth follow for international and global commerce? And what Calendar do
the Stock-Markets, Banks, and Clearing-Houses all follow and pay
out to internationally and globally concerning commerce? – They
follow the Vatican's "Gregorian Calendar", created by pope Gregory.
With the advent of this Calendar, the Vatican has "CAPTURED"
and controls TIME, as well as all of the SHIPPING LANES that
authorize the movement of commerce on Planet Earth; to include
the shipments and movements of all monies and military and therefore, War. Everything moves on the time-lines associated with this
calendar.

In 1775 when the 13 Colonies won their freedom from Great Britain, they were not only penniless but they were bankrupt; owing France to the tune of 1.6 Million Francs. War rages for Seven (7) years. In 1782, they now owe Two-Million Francs to the French. So, the 13 Colonies file for DOMESTIC bankruptcy, as they were not only broke, but war torn as well. On 17 SEPT 1789, The United States cannot pay back, the NOW, Three-Million francs, so England/ "Rothschild" goes ahead and buys the note, throwing The United States into a 70 year INTERNATIONAL Bankruptcy.

There have always been two governments in this country since the end of the American Revolution: The 13 Colonies Republican government and its people, known as the American Nationals who are responsible for creating the Declaration of Independence and the Bill of Rights. The second, is the King of Great Britain's government, who were wealthy Europeans that had come to capitalize on the opportunities of the New World. Such as J.P. Morgan and the Rail-Road Families, who were very much responsible for the push in the creation of the Kings US Constitution. By March of 1788, the King's people had created the US Constitution and in the opinion of the 13 Colonies, it was felt that the document created too strong of a central government and which would eventually usurp the independent rights and power of the peoples state governments in their ability to freely Govern and Censor themselves. When it became clear that the US Constitution

By March of 1788, the King's people had created the US Constitution and in the opinion of the 13 Colonies, it was felt that **the document created too strong of a central government and which would eventually usurp the independent rights and power of the peoples state governments in their ability to freely Govern and Censor themselves.** When it became clear that the US Constitution would be ratified, in an act of National self-preservation and in defense against the Kings US Constitution, the 13 Colonies under the direction of Patrick Henry who was assisted by other anti-Federalists, created and offered 12 Amendments (Bill of Rights) to protect the personal liberties and freedoms of the people of the 13 Colonies. Of these 12 Amendments, 10 were ratified and became the Bill of Rights.

The Bill of Rights was an extension of the Declaration of Independence, which was the only document that contained the immortal signatures of all of the original founding fathers. The Kings US Constitution was never signed by any of the representatives of the 13 Colonies, (except for George Washington, and that is due to the fact that George is a Cousin of the King) nor was it recognized by the 13 Colonies as their form of government. Only with the adoption and recognition of the Bill of Rights by the King's government, did the 13 Colonies quietly agree to ratify the US Constitution and in their quiet disapproval in the face of this document, refused to sign it. However, because the Declaration of Independence had been signed by all of the founders of the 13 Colonies it was attached to the Bill of Rights and then bonded to the US Constitution during the Congressional Assembly which begrudgingly authorized its indirect ratification. With the closing of that Congressional Hearing, the congregation of the general assembly between these two governments, "the Continental Congress of the united States of America" and the municipal corporation, known as "the District of Columbia" - later to become, **"the United States of America inc."** - were to never convene again in the history of this nation. It was over. The Federal Government Services Corporation HAS NEVER held any position of authority over the people of this nation, their rights, or their freedoms in any manner or capacity whatsoever, and never will.

ADMINISTRATIVE HISTORY
Established: Effective June 1, 1871, by an act of February 21, 1871 (16 Stat. 419), abolishing the Corporations of the City of Washington, DC, and Georgetown, DC, and the Levy Court of Washington County, DC; and replacing them with a municipal corporation known as the District of Columbia.

CAVEAT:

("The Declaration of Independence".
Declaration: - "De" = No, "clare" = speak, "at" = location, "ion" = contract.
Independence: - "In" = no, "de" = no, "pend" = write, "ence" = contract.
TRANSLATION (in correct grammatical construct) = "You shall not speak contract and you shall not write contract." - Benjamin Franklin
"The" = ADVERB, "Declaration" = VERB, "of" = ADVERB, making "Independence" = VERB.

Under ~TITLE-18: USCS ~1001 & ~1002, Fictional-Conveyance of Grammar -
~TITLE-15: USCS-1692 E, Fraud/False &: Misleading Statements -

both are false and misleading statements and FICTITIOUS CON-VEYANCE of GRAMMAR. Hence, it is rumored that The Declaration of Independence was auctioned off as a meaningless historical document, written by a French Attorney, who was hired by the English Crown to capture the united States of America, and who was also, in his acting commissions, FOUNDER of the Continental Congress. Welcome to Treason. Eight books have been published on this fact.

CONTINUING: ...

Back to 17 SEPT 1789, add 70 years: Now, NO LAW becomes legal for 90 days. From 17 SEPT, plus a 45 day Trust-Law, plus a 3-day Rescission Act, is the day of the bombing of Fort Sumter in 1860 and the Civil War starts. Add 70 years, 2 NOV 1929, Presidential Election Day, The United States announces that it's coming out of its INTERNATIONAL Bankruptcy. It is called the Year of Jubilee, the forgiving of all debts. However, a 5-Day Rule applies. England alerted The United States of the 5-Day Rule stating that before they were able to close the Banks and Credit-Unions, All banks and Credit-Unions must be given a 5 day notification of the closure. The notice to all Banks and Credit-Unions that they are going to close all banks and Credit-unions on 2 NOV 1929, was posted on 29 OCT 1929, THE DAY THE STOCK-MARKET CRASHED, initiating the great depression. The Dollar was only worth 10-cents globally.

CAVEAT: The Stock-Market crash of 1929 was also an orchestrated interdict over commerce by the Papacy and enacted through the actions of 3 Irish-Roman-Catholic Men: Benjamin Strong, Tom Bragg, and the illustrious Knight of Malta, Joseph P. Kennedy, who were the "SHORT-SELLERS" of the crash. After the interdict, commerce resumed with strictly paper currency; a commercial instrument. Because paper currencies are nothing more than indulgences of the Pope of ROME to engage in commerce, they are backed by nothing, and they are redeemable by nothing.

CONTINUING: ...

So the Bankruptcy was retroactively-renewed to 17 SEPT 1929, add 45-day Trust-Law and you get 2 NOV 1929. Add another 70 years and we arrive at, 2 NOV 1999. Remember the Florida CHADS? The Florida Ballots had to be hand-counted and it took EXACTLY 90 DAYS. WHY? As no law becomes legal for 90 days there are also, **NO LAWS** for 90 days, the I.R.S. does not exist for 90 days, the FEDERAL Government ceased to exist for 90 days and, all contracts between the 50 States and the "Federal Government Services Corporation, aka. "the United States of America inc.", operating out of the District of Columbia, had legally come to an end, were LAWFULLY VACATED and LEGALLY DISSOLVED. With the close-out of the Third and Final International Bankruptcy the "Federal Government Services Corporation, aka. "the United States of America inc.", operating out of the District of Columbia, had to vacate its Postal Contracting Ability as the Post Office for that Corporation. It was for this reason that the U.S. Military, under **the Universal-Postal-Union**, was ordered to DEF-CON 2 as a precautionary tactic should the united States of America be invaded. And on 2 FEB 2000, Bush was appointed as the first C.E.O. and President of <u>PRIVATE</u> Corporate America.

BOTTOM LINE: The Government is the POST-OFFICE folks. the President of the United States [pre-simulation-denture], appoints a POST-MASTER-GENERAL who controls all branches of Government, C.I.A., F.B.I., Police, and Fire. Every branch of government; Homeland-Security, DEPT of Interior, DEPT of Forestry, etc... Everything in the United States is controlled by the Post-Office. The same holds true in other countries. The Kings, Queens and the Rulers & Dictators of the world, are no more than Puppets working for the Post-Master, because the Post-Master controls the Treasury that prints the money and controls the Military that protects and defends the money; or whatever is backing the money, in our case, the land and our GOLD. That is how the world runs.

So, you have to follow the time-lines if you want to know the truth; and these time-lines have been running for roughly 6,700 years.

In 1775 the England Oversight Committee (their Parliament) appointed Benjamin Franklin – who was a French Attorney, working for the English Crown – as a Secret-Agent enacted to capture the united States. (note: the small "u" in united) Where, by working as an English Attorney/Barrister in the united States, he took Jurisdiction of Script (writing Contract) and Money. And when he was eventually voted in as the POST POSTMASTER GENERAL for both the united States and Canada, he was voted in by people who were uneducated in the mechanics of those affairs and led to do so by British loyalists. So later, when he penned the words "We the People", he was using Grammatical Trickery in an effort to accomplish the long range mission of the warfare plan he was hired to conduct, and the Contract Documents that were purposefully drafted as a result were created deceitfully by him, in an act of "Grammar Fraud".

Under Maritime Law, TITLE: 46,-~Ch.,-~1.,-~Sec.,-~1., state's: "The first rule of all Contracts is "CLOSURE". There must be closure for the volition of the Contract, by the initiate. If there is a hidden meaning within ANY CONTRACT, and that meaning [Dictionary Term]was not advertised within that Contract and that meaning, was used for subversive or criminal activity, then that Contract falls under the terminology of, FRAUD." - (:Fraudulent-Parse-Syntax-Grammar.) / [syntax=parts of a word] -

CLOSURE: To provide a person (or position, office of importance) with factual information.

Here's how – When you look at your country's "Styles Manuel" - and every Nation has one – it outlines how letters [syntax] come together to form words in your language and that Styles Manuel is accompanied by a dictionary that provides the definitions of those words, giving you closure on the fact of what that word means. In association with your Periodic Tables and your Elemental Chart – that disclose the temperatures of the static, melting and freezing points of those elements, that in effect convert them from a solid, to a liquid and finally into gas, or vapor - are all bundled together as a GLOBAL CONTRACT containing a grammatical system of Weights & Measures. Wherein is articulated by the measurements of those sums and differences, how it is that your country intends to conduct itself, using this system, in business with the rest of the world.

When Benjamin Franklin wrote, "We the People", as a fiction, he did it to create a Declaration of Independence that was nothing more than an illusion to deceive those whom had entrusted him with such an undertaking.

THE – DECLARATION – OF - INDEPENDENCE

"The", was and Adverb making "Declaration" a Verb, "of" is an Adverb making "Independence", to be a Verb.

"DECLARATION": "De", = No/Separate from. / "clair", = Speak. / "at", = Location. / "ion", = Contract. ---- = No – speak – Contract.

"INDEPENDENCE": "In", = No. / "de", = No/Separate from, / "pen[d]", = scribe. / "ence", = Contract. --- = No – writing – Contract.

THEREFORE = "You shall not speak Contract, you shall not write Contract."

This is what these letters, when placed together [syntax] as they are, mean when you look them up in the 1826 American Dictionary. Which is our Nations Contract Dictionary.

The example of Syntax, or the Parse presented above, in relation to the prefixes and the suffixes used with, or in conjunction to one another to formulate a word, in accordance with their factual meanings as found in the American Dictionary, are presented CORRECTLY,... and every Collegiate and University ENGLISH PhD from every alphabet and clandestine agency on Planet Earth, not only know this truth, but have already substantiated it, long ago.

TO BE CORRECT

In their search to be correct in all forms of communication, these two FEDERAL-POSTAL-JUDGES, began the start of their research all the way back at the inception of all written language, with the study of glyphs and ancient communication through symbols and their meanings. In this process, it was well recognized as they moved forward, that the way we teach grammar and the way in which we use grammar to communicate, are/is erroneous. Through this endeavor to communicate correctly, written or spoken, by these FEDERAL-POSTAL-JUDGES, the correction on all grammar was inadvertently made, globally.

The ensuing mechanical correction on the order of grammatical operations in the articulation of words/grammar precipitately led, serendipitously to the creation of a correct system of mathematically certifiable grammar.

The series of events that have unfolded since that time have been virtually undocumented by ANYONE and formally released into the public sector and are only now, after 20 years, beginning to be recognized and researched by the masses of people on the planet outside of the of the highest levels of Government; where the secret and the power of what this language has done, has been kept in secret, and only spoken of in secret, since the breach.

This is the correction on the mechanical order of operations for all language on planet Earth, and is recognized globally as, the Correct Sentence Structure Communication Parse Syntax Grammar, (C.S.S.C.P.S.G.) - With the now corrected use of grammar and through the articulation of the mathematical interface on this order of operations, a grammatical form of communication based on mathematics was created and has now been introduced globally and recognized by all the leaders of the world in over 200 countries to include those members of the United Nations, the PENTAGON, the U.S. State Department, and the VATICAN, just to name a few; all of the appropriate government agencies have been notified globally, and accept and understand completely what the meaning and power of this correction on language has just accomplished.

The endeavor to be correct in communication by these two Judges continued further, and in that effort with a mathematical interface, they have articulated the construct of a new paradigm and therefore a new position, based on the indisputable universal fact associated with math from which to found and base a new nation and Government form. The creation of this new system of Government is universally founded in a quantum mathematical model. This quantum mathematical model of Government is separate from all other models of Government to have ever been conceived by the mind of man, and in its unique position is manifested in a "Now Time" quantum-scenario-jurisdiction validated by the substantiation of an absolute mathematical fact.

The quantum "Now-Time" communicative construct of this grammar, eliminates any ambiguity in its subjective communicative interpretation by removing all passed, and/or future tense verbiage from the construct of all forms of its communication, and brings the use of grammar into now-time-correctness in a QUANTUM "Now-Time Model" supported by a MATHEMATICAL INTERFACE between itself and Grammar that both authorize and substantiates the communicative standing of this "NOW TIME CORRECTNESS", that in its construction constitutes/grants NOW TIME GRAMMATICAL JURISDICTION – ALL THE TIME – no matter when in "time" the document is revisited ...removing any and all chance for the opportunity of an argument to present itself at a later date in relation to "what it meant when", it was created.

Two days after the publishing and global delivery of this mathematical correction on the use of grammar, the NSA showed up at the doorstep of Judge- : David-Wynn: Miller, and asked Dave, if he and Russell actually realized what it was that they had just done? --- And of course he understood perfectly what they had done, just as well as did the NSA. And, it is PARAMOUNT that you - THE READER – come to understand as well – along with the rest of the world's leaders and intelligence agencies - the GRAVITY of the SIZE, SCOPE and far reaching UNIVERSAL MAGNITUDE, of this UNPRECEDENTED GLOBAL BREACH OF SECURITIES and what it VICTORIOUSLY means to the world at large and finally, to "us" all, as individuals.

What the correction on the use of grammar ultimately accomplished, was the disqualification and destruction of all other forms of grammar on Planet Earth, and in that disqualification, has nullified and destroyed every Contract, Treaty, Trust, & Deed, etc., etc... ever written on Planet Earth within the last 8,500 years between every Nation and every Ruler on Planet Earth, BAR NONE. - AND EVERY GLOBAL LEADER IS AWARE OF IT. --- TO ESPECIALLY INCLUDE THE EMPIRE OF THE 3 CITY STATES and, their Military,… the Militia known as, the Jesuits. Aka, the Knights of Malta and the Royal Order of the Garter.

THIS WAS THE LARGEST BREACH OF GLOBAL SECURITY EVER COMMITTED AND RECORDED IN THE HISTORY OF THE WORLD. - AS IT LITERALLY PUNCHED A HOLE

THROUGH THE VERY FABRIC OF THE CURRENT WORLD
THAT HAS BEEN STRATEGICALLY HELD TOGETHER BY THE
WRITTEN CONTRACTS BETWEEN EVERY COUNTRY AND
EVERY LEADER ON PLANET EARTH. -

CAPTURING THE ORIGINAL NATIVITY LOCATION
FOR BOTH THE POST OFFICE AND
<u>THE ORIGINAL AMERICAN GOVERNMENT</u>

:FACTUAL-QUANTUM-FEDERAL-POSTAL-CONTRACT-
DOCUMENT-AUTHORIZATION

QUANTUM CONTRACT IN C.S.S.C.P.S.G.

EVIDENCE -

1 OCT 2015

:COPYCLAIMS/COPYRIGHTS-~JANUARY-~1980-
THROUGH-~NOW-TIME BY THE PLENIPOTENTIARY-
JUDGE, ~12-~AUGUST-~1999, &: POSTMASTER, &: FED-
ERAL-JUDGE, &: FEDERAL-POSTAL-JUDGE: 21-
~DECEMBER-~2012, PHILADELPHIA-PENNSYLVANIA,
BENJAMIN: FRANKLIN-COURT-OPENING WITH THE
NEW-POSTAL-CHARTER, OATH, CONSTITUTION,
JUDGES-OATH BY THE David-Wynn: Miller AND: POST-
MASTER-GENERAL, &: FEDERAL-POSTAL-COURT-
JUDGE: Russell-Jay: Gould.

FOR THESE 80,000-HOURS OF THE PARSE-SYNTAX-
GRAMMAR and: CORRECT-SENTENCE-STRUCTURE-
COMMUNICATION-PARSE-SYNTAX-GRAMMAR-STUD-
IES OF THE CORRECT-PARSE-SYNTAX-GRAMMAR-LAW-

TRANSLATION WITHIN THE DOCUMENT-CONTRACT-FEDERAL-POSTAL-COURT-VENUE ARE WITH THE DOCUMENT-CLAIM BY THIS FEDERAL-POSTAL-JUDGE: David-Wynn: Miller &: FEDERAL-POSTAL-JUDGE: Russell-Jay: Gould.

FOR THE CORRECT-SENTENCE-STRUCTURE-COMMU-NICATION-PARSE-SYNTAX-GRAMMAR (C.-S.-S.-C.-P.-G.) OF THIS DOCUMENT-CONTRACT-FEDERAL-POSTAL-COURT-VENUE IS WITHIN THESE CLAIMS OR THE DOCUMENT-CONTRACT-FEDERAL-POSTAL-VESSEL-EQUITY-COURT OF THE TWO-OR-MORE-PERSONS WITH THE CONTRACT-VESSEL-CLOSED-DOCUMENT-CONTRACT-FEDERAL-POSTAL-VESSEL-COURT-TERMS BY AN ORIGINAL-PAPER-REGISTERED-MAIL-DOCU-MENT-VENUE.

FOR THE DOCUMENT-PAPER-VESSAL OF THE QUO-WARRANTO-COMPLAINT IS WITHIN THE CLAIM OF THE PAPER-VESSEL-FEDERAL-POSTAL-COURT-VENUE AS THE CLOSED-AREA-VESSEL-COURT WITH THE TERMS OF THE CONSTITUTION-CONTRACT BETWEEN THESE TWO-OR-MORE-PERSONS WITHIN THE DOCU-MENT-CONTRACT-FEDERAL-POSTAL-VESSEL-COURT-VENUE BY THE WRITTEN-EVIDENCE-BONDED (GLUED, STICH, RIVET)-COURT-COMPLAINT-DOCUMENT.

FOR THE TERMS OF A C.-S.-S.-C.-P.-G.-DOCUMENT-CON-TRACT ARE WITH THE TERMS'-CLAIM IN THE DOCU-MENT-CONTRACT-FEDERAL-POSTAL-VESSEL-EQUITY-COURT WITH THE VOID OF AN OUTSIDE-CLAIMS BY A FOREIGN-PAPER, FOREIGN-PARSE-SYNTAX-GRAMMAR-FICTION-LAWS, RULES, CODES, OR: REGULATIONS OF THE MODIFICATION-FICTION-PRONOUN-ADVERB-VERB-SYNTAX-GRAMMAR, ADVERB-ADJECTIVE-PRO-NOUN-SYNTAX-GRAMMAR, ADVERB-VERB-ADVERB-VERB-ADVERB-VERB-SYNTAX-GRAMMAR, OR ADJEC-

TIVE-PRONOUN-SYNTAX-GRAMMAR BY THE FRAUDU-LENT-SYNTAX-GRAMMAR.

:Disclaimer – The timetable(s) associated with the events that took place and are relayed within this report, are not in the actual chronicled order that they factually took place in, but are altered for the purpose of simplifying what happened, and is done in an effort to not complicate the story.

12 DEC 2016

:QUOTE: POSTMASTER-GENERAL: Russell-Jay: Gould.

: I-took-over on the July-12, 2000 with a 93-drougue-law AS THE SOLITARY-POSTMASTER-GENERAL(PASSING-TICKET-CONTRACT AND: SEAL-LETTER OF THE VALUE-BILLS OF THE LADINGS).

: When-federal-government-vacated-D.C. on the 2000-November-presidentual-lection.

: WHICH-VACATES-CONSTITUTION AND: VIOLATE: TITLE:39: 101.

: I-already-know! : Thats-why-fake-postmaster-generals of the united-states-post-office in the D.C., physicalli-run from my now-space, ITS-SO-FUNNY, WATCHING-THOSE-LOSERS-RUN.

: Thats-why-I-could-Military-Court-Marshal: George-Walker: Bush and: Richard-Bruce: Cheney AND: PENTAGON-MILITARY-PERSONS and: Those-bitches-know and: they-know-what-I-call-them and: COURT-MARSHAL-STILL-STANDS.

: POSTMASTER, JOINT-DI-RECTOR AND: FEDERAL-POSTAL-JUDGE: David-Wynn: Miller, is-not-authorized on those bills of the ladings and: he-knows-too.

:**END QUOTE:** POSTMASTER-GENERAL: Russell-Jay: Gould.

BENJAMIN FRANKLIN POST OFFICE
&
THE NATIVITY OF THE US GOVERNMENT

The United-States-Postal-Service lost jurisdiction of its contract-capabilities on 2 NOV 1999 with the end of the 3 rd and final bankruptcy of the United States of America inc.. It then VACATED its Corporate Constitution and VACATED the Trusteeship for the Presidency in the 2000 Florida CHAD Elections.

The Federal Government Services Corporation and ALL of the Federal Employees had to VACATE the rules of the Continuance of the Evidence and physically leave D.C. for 18 days. This was the Florida CHADS, in going outside of the guidelines of the Constitution for the United States of America inc., which DID NOT EXIST ANY LONGER. The Constitution for The United States was held for ransom as a bank-note in relation to the bankruptcy time-line because the grammar was all modified, thereby making it worthless as a real contract-document.

The Federal Government Employees, Obama, etc.. all very cognizant of this fact. But what they were NOT PREPARED FOR was FEDERAL-POSTAL-JUDGE :David-Wynn :Miller, and FEDERAL-POSTAL-JUDGE :Russell-Jay: Gould, positioning themselves as Post-Masters with the correct certifications on the Bills of the Ladings with the C.S.S.C.P.S.G. Contract-Constitution. Which was filed by FEDERAL-POSTAL-JUDGE :Russell-Jay: Gould, under labeling as the Post-Master-General of THE UNITY-STATES OF OUR WORLD-CORPORATION. The United States Postal-Service then vacated its position in compliance with TITLE 39; Sec.101, sub.(a), (b).

94

What that means is that they physically had to leave the District of Columbia for more than 18 days. And that was the scenario that they created because under their Trust Time-lines its a 3 day Rescission, 5 day publication, 10 day communication back, which is 18 days. When they go outside of that parameter they brake the rules of the continuance of the evidence. And that is what they attempted to do with the 2000 Election with a President [Pre-Simulation-Denture] who had no legal assignment of authority to run elections for a CEO and Corporate President to act on behalf of Great Britain in good-faith for the people of the united States of America because it had Legally and Lawfully just been VACATED and ENDED.

That is because this group of Federal Services Employees was about to surrender the united States of America back over to the Crown making everyone in it a Surf or a peasant & slave to fraudulently work off the FICTION debt incurred by the Federal Services Corporation, who is guilty of Racketeering, criminal fraud, banking fraud and Breach of Trust!

From that historical point, Russell and Dave have worked back to that nativity point in time, long ago, and re-opened the original Post-Office of Benjamin Franklin and reconstituted the Declaration of Independence and the Constitution for the united States of America in the C.S.S.C.P.S.G., and in QUANTUM-CONSTRUCT. With that, they have filed for a copyright and a Patent on the TITLE 4,1X1.9 Dimensional Federal Flag of the United States (as one was never filed) and have now captured it and are SAFEGUARDING it, and have kept it from being surrendered over to the N.W.O. They are now holding it for the people of this country. This country was Two-Seconds from being captured and surrendered to the N.W.O., and Commander- :Gould, and FEDERAL-POSTAL-JUDGE :David-Wynn: Miller, STOPPED THE ENTIRE TAKEOVER.

These 2 men. are National Hero's. Sometime after 2 NOV 1999, the usurping federal-Cabal [the N.W.O] became very up-set with COM-MANDER- :Russell-Jay: Gould, because when the Cabal had to vacate the Trusteeship and vacate the District of Columbia, 93 days prior to the surrender, Russell had filed all of his contract-paperwork for his position as POST-MASTER-GENERAL for The United States of America, in the Correct Sentence Structure Communication Parse Syntax Grammar, and in quantum-language, and at that point on 2 NOV 1999, Russell was legally found to be the ONLY VALAD POST-MASTER-GENERAL in The United States of America with a real and valid contract-document, who was legally compliant with: U.S. TITLE-39 (sec. 101, sub-sec - a.) **"All Post-Offices must have a valid Constitution on file."**; Since the U.S. Constitution was being vacated in the Bush & Gore Election of 2000, they [the criminals] then vacated their estate, or their right of usury and Russell's "Bill of the Lading", kicked in.

Which meant that he was now the Legal and Lawful Authority as POST-MASTER-GENERAL to lay the foundation for all of the things which he had Authorized, set into motion, and laid earlier through the POST-OFFICE and back through the Pentagon, giving correct authorizations & delegations, down through those locations thereby keeping the continuance of the evidence in those time-lines. **(Making him the NEW [quiet] Commander-in-Chief for the united States of America)**

This makes FEDERAL-POSTAL-JUDGE :Russell-Jay: Gould the true :FEDERAL-POSTMASTER-GENERAL, COMMANDER-AND-CHIEF of the united States of America; (and then some) and he has been legally holding multiple positions of power, legally keeping the continuance of the evidence for the Post-Office of the united States of America, ever since.

William Henderson, Post Master General for The United States Postal Service, was contacted by FEDERAL-POSTAL-JUDGE :David-Wynn :Miller, and FEDERAL-POSTAL-JUDGE :Russell-Jay: Gould, wherein during a 3 hour briefing and debriefing period it was articulated by William Henderson, that he did not have knowledge of what it was that he was doing as Post Master General for The United States Postal Service and he immediately retired.

96

William J. Henderson: (born June 16, 1947) Served as the United States Postmaster General from May 16, 1998 to June 1, 2001; Henderson is a director of Acxiom Corporation.

Another Post Master General named John Potter, was brought in. On 20FEB 2003, in Washington D.C., there was a scheduled meeting of Post-Masters to convene on that night where FEDERAL-POSTAL-JUDGE :David-Wynn :Miller, and FEDERAL-POSTAL-JUDGE :Russell-Jay: Gould, were going in UNANNOUNCED to meet with these men and inform them of the fact that they were NO LONGER authorized to hold those positions due to the fact that in 1999, with the close of the 3 rd bankruptcy of the Federal Services Corporation, the Trusteeship (Office of President) had to legally be vacated.

Their Corporate Version of their Copyrighted Constitution was vacated and dissolved, all the Federal Employees had to LITERALLY leave D.C. for 18 days and also with the closeout of the 3 rd & Final Bankruptcy the Federal Post Office was closed and with that, Britain's Federal Service Corporation lost its ability to contract with the world as the Post Office representing the people or the country "the united States of America".

With the Vacating of the Federal Government Services Corporation Contracts, **D.C. WAS SURRENDERED** and with that, ALL contract-documents between D.C. and the 50 States were legally ended. There is no British Federal Government Services Corporation Contracts in existence between the 50 States and D.C. any longer and there have not been since 2 NOV 1999..

On that night of the scheduled meeting of Post-Masters, FEDERAL-POSTAL-JUDGE :David-Wynn :Miller, and FEDERAL-POSTAL-JUDGE :Russell-Jay: Gould, had set up a Security-Team of Bounty-Hunters to act as surveillance on their behalf while they were in the building. Half of the Team in the building, half of the Team out of the building. When the "acting" Post Master General, named John Potter walked in through the front door, as soon as FEDERAL-

POSTAL-JUDGE :Russell-Jay: Gould, was identified by John Potter, Potter took off running with his security detail in tow. John Potter and his security detail were secretly followed by the Team of Bounty-Hunters. The Bounty-Hunters now covertly on the elevator with John Potter and his security detail; Potter is quite shaken and anxious. Flustered, he turns to his detail in the elevator and begrudgingly says, - "You guys have got to get me the hell out of here, do you know who that was?? - That was the POST-MASTER-GENERAL of the United States, :Russell-Jay: Gould!" -

This eye-witness information verifies the fact, that the men holding these dissolved contract government services positions, since 1999, have full knowledge that they are doing so illegally as they have no contracts to act on the behalf of the 50 States and are receiving the proceeds and full benefits in relation to that once honorable contracted government station.

John E. "Jack" Potter: (born 1956) Is the President and CEO of the Metropolitan Washington Airports Authority since July 18, 2011. He is the former United States Postmaster General and CEO of the United States Postal Service (USPS), having become the 72nd Postmaster General on June 1, 2001.

The first of many fiction locations that was disqualified and taken down by the Correct Sentence Structure Communication Parse Syntax Grammar (C.S.S.C.P.S.G.) was the Internal Revenue Service on its claim of ownership of your land using FICTION GRAMMAR and FICTION DOCUMENTS that force you to pay "property tax" to them. All of the proper accumulated paper-work was filed in as evidence against the I.R.S.'s claims at the appropriate Court-House. And as all of the legal paper-work was correct and it was complete, the Court-House at that location was ordered open by FEDERAL-POSTAL-JUDGE :Russell-Jay: Gould, wherein the IRS was disqualified and thrown out of the united States of America.

This action was conducted simultaneously and in unison with :FEDERAL-POSTAL-JUDGE :Gould, by FEDERAL-POSTAL-JUDGE

:David-Wynn: Miller, on the Island of Hawaii, as well. This Joint Operation was being initiated and conducted in a legally authorized intelligent effort to "STOP and CORRECT" a SEISIN of a FACT, and because there was knowledge of a SEISIN of a FACT, that knowledge morally obligated these men - out of their responsibility and Duty to act – to Legally take action to lawfully "Stop and Correct" this wrong, incorrect and/or illegal action.

The final judgment in that case with the I.R.S. was in favor of, FEDERAL-POSTAL-JUDGE :Russell-Jay: Gould, and FEDERAL-POSTAL-JUDGE :David-Wynn: Miller. The legal paper-work on those Court Case rulings were then filed and REGISTERED with the Courts, walked out of their respective "Court-House" buildings and further filed and registered around the world with all global positions of Government Authority in both the Civilian and Military sectors through, the Department of Defense, all four branches of the Military, Federal Reserve, U.S Treasury, and the Universal &: U.S. Postal-Union-Service's.

At this point in time FEDERAL-POSTAL-JUDGE :David-Wynn :Miller, and FEDERAL-POSTAL-JUDGE :Russell-Jay: Gould, deployed to Canada and disqualified Canada's Boarder on 30 JUNE 2001. Canada then joins with FEDERAL-POSTAL-JUDGE :David-Wynn :Miller, and FEDERAL-POSTAL-JUDGE :Russell-Jay: Gould's contract. Canada then placed their SEALS on the QUANTUM CONTRACTS of FEDERAL-POSTAL-JUDGE :David-Wynn :Miller, and FEDERAL-POSTAL-JUDGE :Russell-Jay: Gould, where once again these Men were dropped into the well of the Land of CONTRACT in, Calgary Alberta Canada.

This was the, **[Name Redacted]** Case. In this case FEDERAL-POSTAL-JUDGE :Russell-Jay: Gould, was present as the POSTMASTER-GENERAL who disqualified Canada Customs. After literally jumping into the Well-of-the-Court for the inspecting of the Bills of the Ladings in the presence of the Court in this Case, they were found to be 100% fraud and written in fiction grammar. The Presiding Judge then ran out of the Courtroom and brought in the flag of the Court with 3 other Judges now directly behind him.

The recognition of the fiction grammar and the Quantum Construct of the C.S.S.C.P.S.G. were filed between Canada and THE UNITY-STATES OF OUR WORLD-CORPORATION. Those contract-documents were once again filed with, the United Nations, U.S. Customs, Interpol and the Universal Postal Union in BERN Switzerland. At this point, with the judgment of that Court Case Ruling, they created the position of their GLOBAL-BANKING-CONSTI-TUTION, which is a mathematical communication on Quantum-Banking for a Global Currency.

All of this was possible due to the fact that FEDERAL-POSTAL-JUDGE :David-Wynn :Miller, and FEDERAL-POSTAL-JUDGE :Russell-Jay: Gould, proved that the grammatical system of communication we are ERRONEOUSLY teaching, and have ERRONE-OUSLY been taught, has been in absolute error. Again, the University Professors will verify this fact.

FEDERAL-POSTAL-JUDGE :David-Wynn :Miller, and FEDERAL-POSTAL-JUDGE :Russell-Jay: Gould, as JOINT-POST-MASTERS, then turned around and syntaxed the Universal-Postal-Unions Lodial-Title-Claim for property-rights, globally, and filed that, now syntaxed, and thereby proven to be a fraudulent [fiction] document, in the Clearing-House known as, the Universal-Postal-Union. FEDERAL-POSTAL-JUDGE :David-Wynn :Miller, and FEDERAL-POSTAL-JUDGE :Russell-Jay: Gould, then met with the Universal-Postal-Inspectors in BERN, Switzerland on the Universal Postal Contract Documents and the "Clearing-Mechanics" of those foreign vessels. [Post Offices]

In this meeting between the Universal-Postal-Inspectors in BERN, Switzerland, and FEDERAL-POSTAL-JUDGE :David-Wynn :Miller, and FEDERAL-POSTAL-JUDGE :Russell-Jay: Gould, both of these party's were "foreign" to one another in the fact that they hailed from two COMPLETELY SEPARATE JURISDICTIONS, in both Government and Communication. As with the mathematical interface between math and grammar being broken thereby destroying all contracts globally it had to then be used further to create a Quantum Grammatical Construct from whence to found an entire system of Global Government on to properly replace the old system of fraud that the Quantum Construct had just thereby destroyed.

The meeting between these two Separate Jurisdictions was a fundamental necessity in the over-all mission of FEDERAL-POSTAL-JUDGE :David-Wynn :Miller, and FEDERAL-POSTAL-JUDGE :Russell-Jay: Gould, and was being conducted by these two men to ultimately "STOP and CORRECT" a GLOBAL FRAUD, and set up an ENTIRELY NEW WORLD CONSTRUCT IN TRUTH, and in the process along with it, substantiate their own Government founded on this construct, yet in an entirely separate and SOVERIGN Paradigm, from a mathematically certifiable QUANTUM position, as with the correction on grammar all positions on Earth have thereby been disqualified and destroyed and MUST BE RECONSTITUTED, correctly by FEDERAL-POSTAL-JUDGE :David-Wynn :Miller, and FEDERAL-POSTAL-JUDGE :Russell-Jay: Gould.

QUOTE: FEDERAL-POSTAL-JUDGE :Russell-Jay: Gould

: Concerning-Parties:

: Disqualified-grammar: TITLE-~18: 1001: FICTITIOUS-GRAMMAR on the "Brenton Woods Institutions, BRENTON=ADJECTIVE=DOG OR FROG OR TAPE OR ECT....., WOODS=ADJECTIVE=SOCK or TREE or GLASS, INSTITUTION=PRONOUN=NO-FACT" "all-Letters of Intent"=letter=pronoun, Of-adverb-intent=verb, which-is-fraud, IN=stitution as a prefix-to-any-word-means-NO."
: How-do-you-have-duty for any banking in a negative-nothing?, answer:
: David-Wynn: Miller &: I-disqualified-postal-banking-mechanics for the movement of the banking-tools at the "POSTAL-BANKING-Clearing-House-Universal Postal Union-BILLS=PRONOUN OF=ADVERB LADING=VERB=NO-SUCH-THING",=global-

banking-system on the bills of the ladings-disqualified-GRAMMAR.
: Postmaster-General: Russell-Jay: Gould, TOOK-OVER-WHEN-U.S.-came-out of a 70-year-[in]ternational-bankruptcy-~2- ~November-~1999, End-U.S.-CONSTITUTION AND U.S.P.S.-BANKING-AUTHORIZATION. : FEDERAL-GOVERNMENT-VACATED ON THE PRESIDENTIAL-ELECTION-~2000, NO-U.S.-AUTHORIZATION IN THE GLOBAL-BANKING, JUST-ILLUSION. :82-nations at the united-nations-gave-our-bank-charter for each countries-treasury-~2003-Winter/Spring.

: We-did-it-postal-corporate, so-stands.
: Anybody-doing-"letters of intent"-is-bullshit, stay-away.

: FEDERAL-POSTAL-JUDGE, POSTMASTER-GENERAL &: DIRECTOR: Russell-Jay: Gould.

END QUOTE: FEDERAL-POSTAL-JUDGE :Russell-Jay: Gould

That means that the Jurisdiction of the Universal-Postal-Inspectors in BERN, Switzerland, DOES NOT EXIST, as it is now considered "fiction" due to both their syntax and their grammar. They are writing in a "future-tense" and "past-tense" fiction form of communication. The past is gone and no-one knows the future; it's a "craps-shoot"; none of it exists in the world of FACT where written contract-documents are concerned.

Wherewith, at the close of these proceedings between the Universal-Postal-Inspectors in BERN, Switzerland, the Lodial and Title property claim for the jurisdiction of "all the Land on Planet Earth" had just been transferred over to the Quantum Command and Control of the new Universal-Postmaster-General of the World, :Russell-Jay: Gould.

Since long before 1999, that has been the Overall Objective of their Mission. The whole Global System of Control – that was set up by Criminals as a Criminal Empire under the Command and Control of Criminals - needed to be LEGALLY and LAWFULLY replaced because the long range objective of this Criminal Syndicate is to SLAUGHTER 2/3rds of THE WORLDS HUMAN POPULATION. And the grammar was the key in defeating the ENTIRE SYSTEM and because the Grammar that they have taught us all to adopt and accept is constructed wrong, it has been being used in every effort conceivable to beguile and harvest the people using it in order to defraud us right out of our right to live on the Planet. Whereby the OVERALL OBJECTIVE of their WARFARE PLAN to say that they OWN THE WHOLE PLANET and EVERYTHING ON IT; TO IN-CLUDE YOU. And with that, your slaughter will ensue.

At this point, with the judgment of the :[**Name Redacted**] Case. Court Case Ruling, they created the position of their GLOBAL-BANKING-CONSTITUTION, which is a mathematical communi-cation on Quantum-Banking for a Global Currency, which was pre-sented to the I.M.F. and the World Bank by, FPJ :Gould and :Miller. While at the I.M.F. FEDERAL-POSTAL-JUDGE :Russell-Jay: Gould, placed his Silver and Gold filings out on the table. The Gold and Silver represented a TRUE value and as the Senior Team at the I.M.F. read the contracts, they were overwhelmed with absolute fear and at that moment, as FEDERAL-POSTAL-JUDGE :Russell-Jay: Gould jumped to stand-up he said, -

"And now, I am paying Myself to be the Owner and GLOBAL-BANK BANKER, of this facility; because I know that you ALL have Birth-Certificates and none of you Legally exist; it's all fraud and therefore I'm walking right through your FICTION ILLUSION." -

AND WITH THAT, (and all of the other stuff prior, and to come) The WORLD BANK was DISQUALIFIED as a FICTION SYSTEM and CAPTURED) by, :WORLD-BANK BANKER, :FEDERAL-POSTAL-JUDGE :Russell-Jay: Gould.

So with that being said, in regard to the mechanical correction on the order of grammatical operations, now supported by a mathematical interface from which to substantiate a factual point of communica-

103

tive reference from, everything on the planet needed to be reconstituted in the Correct Sentence Structure Communication Parse Syntax Grammar (C.S.S.C.P.S.G.) and further more, in a QUANTUM CONSTRUCT.

:FEDERAL-POSTAL-JUDGE :David-Wynn :Miller, and :FEDERAL-POSTAL-JUDGE :Russell-Jay: Gould, then went on to the United Nations and legged in with 82 nations and presented their Quantum GLOBAL Bank Charters to the World as the new owners the WORLD BANK in factual position and from a mathematically factual CORRECT Quantum Global Government Construct.

SEISIN : (or seizin) denotes the legal possession of a feudal fiefdom or fee, that is to say an estate in land. It was used in the form of "the son and heir of X has obtained seisin of his inheritance", and thus is effectively a term concerned with conveyancing in the feudal era.

This is what gave FEDERAL-POSTAL-JUDGE :David-Wynn :Miller, and FEDERAL-POSTAL-JUDGE :Russell-Jay: Gould, Carte' – Blanch to stop and correct in recognition of any crime. As they had all knowledge and authority, they walked into the U.S. Treasury on 15 JANUARY 2002 and commanded them to take down the Flag at that location. The Flag that they were flying at the U.S. Treasury Office was not to be registered or recognized anywhere in the world. It was a 1 X 1.25 Dimension FRAUDULENT-FICTION-CHILDRENS-PLAYGROUND-FLAG and it was disrespectfully flying illegally in a position in fraud. That is because FEDERAL-POSTAL-JUDGE :David-Wynn :Miller, and FEDERAL-POSTAL-JUDGE :Russell-Jay: Gould, had already legally captured the REAL, TITLE 4: 1 X 1.9 Dimension Federal Flag of the United States of America.

At this juncture, all of the Treasury Agents were kicked out and the head of US Secret Service was brought in, who specifically told FEDERAL-POSTAL-JUDGE :David-Wynn :Miller, and FEDERAL-POSTAL-JUDGE :Russell-Jay: Gould, that, "it is CORPORATE POLICY of the UNITED STATES GOVERNMENT TO HIRE STU-

PID PEOPLE. In that way the people on top are not accountable for what those dummy's do".

The US Secret Service then recognized FEDERAL-POSTAL-JUDGE :David-Wynn :Miller, and FEDERAL-POSTAL-JUDGE :Russell-Jay: Gould and proceeded to lower the fraudulent flag that they had flying and replaced it with the proper TITLE 4: 1 X 1.9 Dimension Quantum-Grammar-Flag at that time. This is "Old Glory"; the flag that FEDERAL-POSTAL-JUDGE :David-Wynn :Miller, and FEDERAL-POSTAL-JUDGE :Russell-Jay: Gould, have captured to safeguard.

It is now registered as the Grammar-Flag of THE UNITY-STATES OF OUR WORLD-CORPORATION, and it is the only flag that flies "front and center" amongst all of the other flags at the United Nations and is known as the C.S.S.C.P.S.G. Quantum-Language Grammar-Flag.

(it was articulated by FEDERAL-POSTAL-JUDGE :Russell-Jay: Gould, that it was unfortunate that the Treasury was keeping its employees dumbed down and further proceeding to engage in illegal activity)

20 FEB 2003 FEDERAL-POSTAL-JUDGE :David-Wynn :Miller, and FEDERAL-POSTAL-JUDGE :Russell-Jay: Gould, filed in as Joint-Muster-Masters through the Secretary of the Navy's Office as the "Super-intendants of grammar Fraud" within the construct contracts of the U.S. PENTAGON for all Soldiers that were Postal-Employee-Soldiers and that were attached to their subsidiary Military branches. (Army, Navy, etc..)

This was all done prior to and for the purpose of syntaxing the Electoral College Votes Grammar syntax, for the ADVERB-VERB World, on the ballots themselves, which was found to be all fiction grammar and therefore fake. FEDERAL-POSTAL-JUDGE :David-Wynn :Miller, and FEDERAL-POSTAL-JUDGE :Russell-Jay: Gould, then turned around and filed those fraudulent syntaxed ballots with all 50

States because all 50 States were at war because none of them had their own money. They are all currently borrowing money from the I.M.F. & WORLD BANK because the States themselves are broke.

None of them have their own fee for freight for the Bills of the Ladings. With the disqualification of the Electoral College Voting Ballots Grammar syntax, it has been proven that no election has been conducted correctly and the States have been alerted to the fact that until the grammar is corrected, there can be NO ELECTIONS held. Not to mention, the Federal Corporation can never join any elections with the 50 States in an attempt to represent us globally in any National affairs of State or in any other capacity for that matter, ever again. Their fraudulent illegal reign of fraud is over.

FEDERAL-POSTAL-JUDGE :David-Wynn :Miller, and FEDERAL-POSTAL-JUDGE :Russell-Jay: Gould, were then authorized as the certifying body on all contract-documents and that authorization became the equity for their Quantum-Program Grammar-Flag to be lodged and journaled at the Secretary of the Elections Commission for each Territory and each State. Further they then filed as a foreign condition of the State through the United States Office of the Department of State, as a condition of the State for grammar certification and a condition of State for flags. The Flag gave it the authorization, because the rules for the continuance of the evidence, in relation to the continued standing of the united States of America and its Post-Office, had been maintained by FEDERAL-POSTAL-JUDGE :David-Wynn :Miller, and FEDERAL-POSTAL-JUDGE :Russell-Jay: Gould, thereby keeping the nation and its flag in good continued standing and, safe from surrender and/or capture by any other Nation or power on Earth.

In April 2003, FEDERAL-POSTAL-JUDGE :David-Wynn :Miller, and FEDERAL-POSTAL-JUDGE :Russell-Jay: Gould, then met with head of the Postal Administration for The United Nations, Robert Grey, who was very eager to meet these Men, and upon their meeting shook their hands and said, -

" It's a great pleasure to meet you FEDERAL-POSTAL-JUDGES :Gould and :Miller, you are the greatest Post-Masters on the Planet! - We know exactly who you guys are." -

Robert Grey was then asked to verify the United Nations authorization and present the credentials for the existence of the United Nations in the C.S.S.C.P.S.G. It was then explained to FEDERAL-POSTAL-JUDGE :David-Wynn :Miller, and FEDERAL-POSTAL-JUDGE :Russell-Jay: Gould, by Postal Administrator, Robert Grey, that the United Nations did not have any Legal Contracts whatsoever to operate or exist as a Corporation and further they could not read or write properly in the C.S.S.C.P.S.G. and were now going to Contract with THE UNITY-STATES OF OUR WORLD-CORPORATION, to be its Student.

Postal Administrator, Robert Grey was quoted as saying, "You will keep us safe from ourselves."

From here FEDERAL-POSTAL-JUDGE :David-Wynn :Miller, and FEDERAL-POSTAL-JUDGE :Russell-Jay: Gould, went to Interpol where the proper Policing of grammar and what it means in contract-documents was discussed, and further what that means for all of the nations and for world security. Interpol's position and what their role was in relation to all of this was discussed at great length. FEDERAL-POSTAL-JUDGE :David-Wynn :Miller, and FEDERAL-POSTAL-JUDGE :Russell-Jay: Gould, then syntaxed Interpol's Constitution and as it was found to be written in fiction and 100% Fraud, wherein it was rewritten in QUANTUM-GRAMMAR and posted it with them whereby they have a position of correctness from which to found and base their global security operations from.

WASHINGTON DC

In 2005, they then proceeded to deploy to Washington D. C. to disqualify and take-down the U.S. Supreme Court. On that day 12 Marshals were dispatched by the Justices in the Supreme Court Building to stand on the first step to the Court House to force FEDERAL-

POSTAL-JUDGE :David-Wynn :Miller, and FEDERAL-POSTAL-JUDGE :Russell-Jay: Gould to conduct their Court Proceedings on the side-walk in front of the Supreme Court Building. The reason for that is the Supreme Court Justices knew that these FEDERAL-POSTAL-JUDGES were 100% correct in everything that they were doing and feared for their own arrests.

However, as Divine Providence would continue to manifest itself, one of the 12 Marshals lost his balance and stepped off of the first step and onto the side-walk. Wherein, now out of his jurisdiction and on the same plane as the AMERICAN-FEDERAL-POSTAL-JUDGES, he was captured, Deputized, Tip-Staffed [made to work for a superior authority] and ordered to hold the Real Title 4, 1x1.9 dimension Federal (G-Spec) Government Flag for the united States of America for 2 hours. All the while the 9 Supreme Court Justices were lawfully Prosecuted for failing to have a Correct/Factual Oath of Office, a Drogue-Law, Sea-Pass and/or a See-Treaty to even Dock the vessel of the "Supreme Court Building" on planet Earth. Furthermore they were found guilty of Trespassing, Extortion, Coercion, Racketeering, Embezzlement, Fraud, Strong-Armed Robbery, Impersonating Officers of the Court, International Espionage, Terrorist Activity and Terrorism as illegal Foreign Invaders. Whereby they had NO AUTHORITY nor LEGAL STANDING, nor LAWFUL POWER to enforce their private copyrighted fiction system of international codes & statutes of their own copyrighted Public Opinion on a nation of people they had NO LEGAL or LAWFUL JURISDICTION OVER.

The entire Supreme Court System has no CORRECT AUTHORIZATIONS of any kind to be anywhere within the United States of America to conduct its acts of Inland Piracy against the free people of the 50 Territories. Not to mention that with the Office of the Trustee being LEGALLY Vacated in 1999 UNDER INTERNATIONAL/GLOBAL BANKRUPTCY LAW, they further have no standing for recognition of any kind by the people of the united States.

The captured Marshal was then ordered to carry the documents of criminal prosecution into the building of fraudulent Supreme Court House and file them. Where upon once those documents of criminal prosecution were filed, it legally concluded the Criminal Hearing, Prosecution and Sentencing of the largest criminal court syndicate of criminal imposter's by this nations First and most powerful FACTUAL pair of Sovereign, SUPREME-FEDERAL-POSTAL-JUDGES to have ever been LEGALLY Authorized and LAWFULLY Enacted in the historical founding of the united States of America.

Once the notification was correctly filed the 9 Judges took their positions in the Court-Room on their benches and then invited FEDERAL-POSTAL-JUDGE :David-Wynn :Miller, and FEDERAL-POSTAL-JUDGE :Russell-Jay: Gould, to come in. But according to the 15 Minute Tardy Rule, the Court was ordered open at 0900hrs and since none of the Judges showed up at that time to open the Court, as ordered, they were disqualified and FEDERAL-POSTAL-JUDGE :David-Wynn :Miller, and FEDERAL-POSTAL-JUDGE :Russell-Jay: Gould, then declared that they no longer needed the Court as there were no Judges in it, AND AT THAT POINT IT WAS LEGALLY and LAWFULLY CLOSED DOWN here in THE UNITY-STATES OF OUR WORLD-CORPORATION "the united States of America", by them,… for good. As they have No Authorization, they have No Standing, and as they have No Standing, they therefore are Defunct and do not exist.

However, as a caveat to this, –- later after filing and closing the Supreme Court down here in the united States of America, FEDERAL-POSTAL-JUDGE :David-Wynn :Miller, and FEDERAL-POSTAL-JUDGE :Russell-Jay: Gould, (hereafter::Miller &: Gould) entered the Court House and ordered the Supreme Court Justices to come down from off of their benches and join them on a common plane. The Supreme Justices refused and with that, they were identified by :Miller &: Gould, as nothing more than "ACTORS" on a stage impersonating Officers of the Court. :Miller &: Gould, then turned their backs on those criminal imposter's and walked out of the Court-Room.

Within 24 hours, Seven of the Justices resigned.

QUOTE: FEDERAL-POSTAL-JUDGE :Russell-Jay: Gould

~0: Concerning-PERSONS,

~1: U.S.-Federal-Courts-Closed and: State-Courts-Closed, Cause of the Martial-Law, Follow-Contract-Methods of the Flags &: Flag-Standards, Which-Set: VENUES. (: MILITARY-SPIRE-HOISTS IN EACH STATE-GOVERNORS-[OF]FICE-WHICH-SUSPENDS-STATE-CONSTITUTIONS IN EACH STATE, EAGLE-FLAG-STANDARDS, [DE]PENDING OF THE WAY-EAGLE-WINGS-ARE, GIVE-CLOSURES ON WHAT VENUE-YOUR-IN-~VATICAN-WARS OR: POSTAL-WARS.)

~2: I-dis-qualified-U.S.-Supreme-Court-Authorization-~1-~October-~2004, that's-waste of the time. (: U.S.-SUPREME-COURT-PO-LICE-JOINER &: U.S.-MARSHAL-JOINDERS, JOINT-CHIEF-FEDERAL-POSTAL-JUDGE: David-Wynn: Miller's-CORPORA-TION-JOINER.)

≈3: U.S.-Military-Dis-Qualified, When, Postal-Military-Personal-Register with the Federal-Postal-System before they Join-MILITARY, U.S.-POSTAL-SERVICE-AUTHORIZATION-ENDED, VOILATION-~TITLE-~39: SECTION-~101, FAKE-PRESIDEN-TIAL-ELECTION-~2000, VACATE-U.S.-CONSTITUTION-BANKRUPTCY-NOTE, ENDED-U.S.-MILITARY-PERSONAL-AUTHORIZATIONS &: ENDED-U.S.-POSTAL-SERVICE-AU-THORIZATIONS &: ENDED-U.S.-CONSTITUTION-GUIDE-LINES WITH THE KNOWLEDGE BY THE U.S.-[AD]MINISTRATIVE-COURT-HEADS, U.S.-POSTAL-SERVICE-HEADS &: U.S.-MILITARY-HANDLERS(CREATES-ALLING-WARS/POSTAL-PLOYEES/U.S.-MILITARY-MEMEBERS).(: THATS-WHY-CORPORATE-POLICY OF THE U.S.-GOVERN-MENT FOR THE HIRING OF THE STUPID-PEOPLE-QUOTE BY THE HEAD OF THE U.S.-SECRET-SERVICE, 4-FLO0R-U.S.-TREASURY-~CLASSIFIED-CONVERSATION-~15-~JANUARY-

~2002 BETWEEN THE U.S.-SECRET-SERVICE-HEAD, WIT-NESS-CLAIMANT-POSTMASTER: David-Wynn: Miller &: POST-MASTER-GENERAL: Russell-Jay: Gould.)

~4: DIRECTOR, FEDERAL-POSTAL-JUDGE, JOINT-CHIEF-FEDERAL-POSTAL-JUDGE(: David-Wynn: Miller-JOINT-CHIEF-JUDGE-CORPORATION), POSTAL-[IN]SPECTOR, POSTMAS-TER-BANK-BANKER, VATICAN-CITY-KEY-MASTER, WORLD-CENTRAL-BANK-OWNER, PRIZE-MASTER, PRIZE-COMMISSIONER, COMPTROLLER OF THE GLOBAL-FOR-EIGN-POSTAL-CURRENCY, POSTMASTER-GENERAL, PEN-TAGON-PAYMASTER-GENERAL, MUSTER-MASTER-GEN-ERAL, MUSTER-MASTER--NAVY, COMMAND &: CHIEF: Russell-Jay: Gould.

END QUOTE: FEDERAL-POSTAL-JUDGE :Russell-Jay: Gould

This is a testimony to the reality of what these men have accomplished, and those working in the highest realms of this establishment, that sit upon seats of inscrutable power, know that FEDERAL-POSTAL-JUDGE :David-Wynn :Miller, and FEDERAL-POSTAL-JUDGE :Russell-Jay: Gould, are 100% correct with everything that they are doing, and they know that they are doing it for this Nation and its people and to end the "Administrative" Tyranny operating out of Washington DC, against them. Shortly after the routing of the Supreme Court Justices, :Miller &: Gould, prosecuted the England Over-Sight Committee for appointing Benjamin Franklin as a FED-ERAL-POSTAL-JUDGE, in Fiction with a Fiction Order and reprimanded them under TITLE 42 1986; for knowledge of a crime. And TITLE 18 1001; fictitious conveyance of language; false and misleading statements, and depervation of rights, under "coloring of the law". Because FEDERAL-POSTAL-JUDGE :David-Wynn :Miller, and FEDERAL-POSTAL-JUDGE :Russell-Jay: Gould, had the signed confessions of their criminal activity, via' the Committee's conduct, and as all of it was engineered and not an accident, all of the correct paper-work of the :FEDERAL-POSTAL-JUDGES, that had been filed in the Correct Grammar at the location of the

Benjamin Franklin Post Office and abroad by FEDERAL-POSTAL-JUDGE :David-Wynn :Miller, and FEDERAL-POSTAL-JUDGE :Russell-Jay: Gould, then had complete legal and lawful jurisdiction over and above the England Over-Sight Committee, and their contract-document fiction-grammar fraudulent illusions.

TRIP TO THE VATICAN

Over the course of 20 years, these Federal-Judges have cut their teeth on victory after victory, while at war with criminality in the government trenches here in the United States. Most of the wars fought by FEDERAL-POSTAL-JUDGE :David-Wynn :Miller, and FEDERAL-POSTAL-JUDGE :Russell-Jay: Gould, were fought protecting this country and the free people of the 50 Territories.

This is where they take their mission to the highest level on Earth and deploy themselves into Vatican City to conduct further operations. These operations were centered around a Treaty and involved ALL other Treaties. The See-Treaty is a Treaty that entails getting permission from the Vatican/Papacy to do something that allows him to "see" what it is that you or your government might me doing. (not to be confused with a SEA-PASS)

FEDERAL-POSTAL-JUDGE :David-Wynn :Miller, and FEDERAL-POSTAL-JUDGE :Russell-Jay: Gould, deployed to the Vatican to give closure on the articulation and definition of a LIGHT-HOUSE-TREATY under Obelisk-Triangulation authorization and knowledge. (Classified)

FEDERAL-POSTAL-JUDGE :David-Wynn :Miller, and FEDERAL-POSTAL-JUDGE :Russell-Jay: Gould, then filed a SEE-TREATY and identified the syntax, as what they could see. The character symbol usuries of the alphabet, the character symbol usuries of the mechanics of "SIGN", "CO-SIGN", "+", "-", etc, etc.. and the mathematical equals sign (=) to create Sums and Differences were identified. Also identified were the fee's for freight for postal-stamps as they authorize the ability to move the vessel-contracts as well as the flags. FEDERAL-POSTAL-JUDGE :David-Wynn :Miller, and FED-ERAL-POSTAL-JUDGE :Russell-Jay: Gould, met with Cardinal Angelo Sodano, the Secretary of the States Office at the Vatican, where the log-books to enter into their foreign vessel in dry-dock [the Vatican] were syntaxed and found to be fraud.

FEDERAL-POSTAL-JUDGE :David-Wynn :Miller, and FEDERAL-POSTAL-JUDGE :Russell-Jay: Gould, then logged in their SEA-PASS and their Post-Road-Treaty's with the Post-Office nearest the Diplomatic-Consoler-Post of the Vatican-City. The Vatican-City itself, because it was cognizant of how addresses work to create bank-ledger-debt for all homes and locations on the planet, armed with that knowledge, positioned themselves under a GPS location of Astrological-Space-Coordinates, thereby removing themselves from any system that could potentially enslave them in the same manner and fashion that the rest of the world is enslaved to. One small problem with all of that and has to do with the construction of the Vatican and the mathematical formula's used by Michael Angelo throughout its design.

Saint Peters Basilica was accidentally constructed in error, the error by M. Angelo was that the mathematical sequence and the construct used to create their light-energy obelisk triangulations for the shipments and movement of matter was erroneously built in the shape of a dome out of concrete. The problem with that, is that Earth is a vessel itself floating through a sea of space moving through time and space as well, for the proper authorization to constitute the contract triangulation claims, the dome should have been made of glass, or left open. Then the light coming down could properly pass through the mechanical Masonic-Rituals to authorize the creation of their compass-roads and their lay-lines in association with the mechanics of what they were doing. Basically, GOD could enter and they could in turn, commune with GOD at that location.

Also when the Vatican was built by M. Angelo he failed to realize that everything in the Universe is in motion, and the math and coordinates that he used to construct Vatican its lay-lines locked the

Vatican into that time-space location permanently, disqualifying it for any later contractual authorizations once its astrological alignments were lost, as they now have been.

Due to the articulated full closure of what FEDERAL-POSTAL-JUDGE :David-Wynn :Miller, and FEDERAL-POSTAL-JUDGE :Russell-Jay: Gould, were seeing in relation to the Vatican's design, and in regard to Saint Peters Cathedral on the lay-lines, the Gargoyles and the Basilisks holding the sands of time in a horizontal position(hour-glasses) and in recognition of the Caiaphas, they were very cognizant that it was a position on Earth to CONTROL TIME. FEDERAL-POSTAL-JUDGE :David-Wynn :Miller, and FEDERAL-POSTAL-JUDGE :Russell-Jay: Gould, then filed in as KEY-MASTERS of that location so that anybody that was doing business with the Vatican could not be in joinder with its fiction position and as Vatican-City Key-Masters, this gave FEDERAL-POSTAL-JUDGE :David-Wynn :Miller, and FEDERAL-POSTAL-JUDGE :Russell-Jay: Gould, SOLITARY COMMAND &: CONTROL of the grammar on all of the Vaticans contracts.

The Secretary of the States Office at the Vatican concurred with what FEDERAL-POSTAL-JUDGE :David-Wynn :Miller, and FEDERAL-POSTAL-JUDGE :Russell-Jay: Gould, had said and surrounded them with a fleet of cardinals and Bishops who walked/escorted them around the foyers and furthermore walked around identifying the lay-lines and all of the Tom-Foolery connected with that, and they concurred that FEDERAL-POSTAL-JUDGE :David-Wynn :Miller, and FEDERAL-POSTAL-JUDGE :Russell-Jay: Gould, were the two Men that had punched a hole through their entire system of global control and LEGALLY disqualified it globally.

Due to this fact, FEDERAL-POSTAL-JUDGE :David-Wynn :Miller, and FEDERAL-POSTAL-JUDGE :Russell-Jay: Gould, have been given full authorization, as Corporate, witnesses, and Post-Master-Bank-Bankers, to correct the Styles of grammar within the construct of all of the documents created for those doing business with Vatican City, and because it is a fraudulent location using fraudulent grammar, further means that the Vatican holds no assignment of authority to do anything on the planet with anyone. –

In response to this visit to the Vatican by FEDERAL-POSTAL-JUDGE :David-Wynn :Miller, and FEDERAL-POSTAL-JUDGE :Russell-Jay: Gould, that Pope who was present during the visit was removed from office and he later died, the Clergy then vacated the position of the conclave of Vatican City, filing their Postal-Contracts in 19 days instead of on the proper18 days, which has always fallen on the publication day of the chosen Pope. Which then broke the rules of the continuance of the evidence for their "SEE", and the Vatican surrendered all Global-Contract-Authorization to FEDERAL-POSTAL-JUDGE :David-Wynn :Miller, and FEDERAL-POSTAL-JUDGE :Russell-Jay: Gould, and granted complete authorization to use the Obelisk-Triangulations to move all Militaries, Commerce and Contracts from point "A" to point "Z" on this entire planet, to include the galaxy if they went galactic using FEDERAL-POSTAL-JUDGE :David-Wynn :Miller, and FEDERAL-POSTAL-JUDGE :Russell-Jay: Gould's, Galactic-Postal-Union System, that is filed and registered in the C.S.S.C.P.S.G. as part of their Quantum-Global-Government-Construct. It is the only one in existence and was created for the Space-Program and our future endeavors in its exploration and colonization.

So the rules for the continuance of the evidence were broke in relation to the conclave of Vatican City, and moved to 19 days, and when that Pope was removed from office they then preformed a 3 and 10 day (3 day Rescission, 10 day communication back) Postal Maneuver, thereby joining with their "no authorization" fiction-position to create a "no authorization" fiction-position for a Fiction Pope who has no authorization to act in any capacity; legal or other-wise, any-where on the planet.

That is why the BLACK-POPE – the GENERAL of the Jesuit Militia, aka Vatican Military High Command – has taken over Command and Control of the Vatican and Vatican City. And as he is a Military General (bestowed with more authority than the Pope) and NOT A

PONTIFF (whatever that is) he is not a real member of the clergy,... and would therefore be nothing short of a false profit were he to open his mouth and utter a single word in relation to GOD, GOD'S Plans, JESUS or the Angels.

CAVEAT:

Since 2003, the US Military has been used to respond as the "Big-Stick" to everything that has been initiated by the Vatican. One need look no further than the death of Muammar Gaddafi. For 41 years until his demise in October 2011, Muammar Gaddafi did some truly amazing things for his country and repeatedly tried to unite and empower the whole of Africa.

1. In Libya a home is considered a natural human right
In Gaddafi's Green Book it states: "The house is a basic need of both the individual and the family, therefore it should not be owned by others". Gaddafi's Green Book is the formal leader's political philosophy, it was first published in 1975 and was intended reading for all Libyans even being included in the national curriculum.

2. Education and medical treatment were all free
Under Gaddafi, Libya could boast one of the best healthcare services in the Middle East and Africa. Also if a Libyan citizen could not access the desired educational course or correct medical treatment in Libya they were funded to go abroad.

3. Gaddafi carried out the world's largest irrigation project
The largest irrigation system in the world also known as the great manmade river was designed to make water readily available to all Libyan's across the entire country. It was funded by the Gaddafi government and it said that Gaddafi himself called it "the eighth wonder of the world".

4. It was free to start a farming business
If any Libyan wanted to start a farm they were given a house, farm land and live stock and seeds all free of charge.

5. A bursary was given to mothers with newborn babies
When a Libyan woman gave birth she was given 5000 (US dollars) for herself and the child.

6. Electricity was free
Electricity was free in Libya meaning absolutely no electric bills!

7. Cheap petrol
During Gaddafi's reign the price of petrol in Libya was as low as 0.14 (US dollars) per litre.

8. Gaddafi raised the level of education
Before Gaddafi only 25% of Libyans were literate. This figure was brought up to 87% with 25% earning university degrees.

9. Libya had It's own state bank
Libya had its own State bank, which provided loans to citizens at zero percent interest by law and they had no external debt.

... IT'S OWN BANK, NO DEBT, NO INTEREST, FREE TO FARM,... And they MURDERED GADDAFI,... why,... because we all know that no one does anything for free and everything you do here on Planet Earth, is a PRIVILEGE that is only granted to you, by the "Pope" himself. (Insanity.) - - And as DIRECTOR VATICAN-CITY-BANKING/WORLD-BANK-OWNER/GLOBAL-MON-ETARY-FUND-OWNER/COMMANDER/CHIEF/MUSTER-MAS-TER/KEY-MASTER: Russell-Jay: Gould, has taken FACTUAL Command and Control of those positions, those acting as though they hold them, are doing so in an act of fraud.-

END CAVEAT -

Again, follow the time-lines. Everything is right in front of you, if you know how to cypher the codes of banking.

QUOTE: FEDERAL-POSTAL-JUDGE :Russell-Jay: Gould :Vatican-banking-void-authorization, :Director-Vatican-City-Banking/Key-Master: Russell-Jay: Gould, June-~16-~2003-COMMERCIAL-BOOK-IN-TREATY BETWEEN THE VATICAN-CITY-SECRETARY OF THE STATE'S-POSTAL-POSTAGE-STAMP-CANCELLATIONS AND: DIRECTOR VATICAN-CITY-BANKING/WORLD-BANK-OWNER/GLOBAL-MONETARY-FUND-OWNER/COMMANDER/CHIEF/MUSTER-MASTER/KEY-MASTER: Russell-Jay: Gould's-VATICAN-CITY-POSTAGE-STAMP-AUTOGRAPH AND: POSTAL-STAMP-CANCELLATIONS.

:VATICAN-CITY-BANKING, NEEDS-MY-FINGER-PRINT &: QUANTUM-GRAMMAR-WRITING ON THE BANK-CONTRACT FOR THE FOREIGN-VATICAN-BANK-CONTRACT AS THE CORRECT FOR A BANKING-PERFORMANCE BY THE FOREIGN-POSTMASTERS-BANKS-BANKERS.

:VATICAN-FOREIGN-BANKING-POSTMASTER-PERSONS-KNOW, WHAT'S-UP.

:WITH THIS HONOR: VATICAN-CITY-BANKING-DIRECTOR/VATICAN-CITY-~EUROPE-KEY-MASTER, COMMANDER &: CHIEF: Russell-Jay: Gould.

END QUOTE: FEDERAL-POSTAL-JUDGE :Russell-Jay: Gould

FOUND TO BE 100% CORRECT
and
- :GLOBAL-COMMANDER-AND-CHIEF: -

Before this quest to create his own System of Government started out, :DIRECTOR, FEDERAL-POSTAL-JUDGE, JOINT-CHIEF-FEDERAL-POSTAL-JUDGE, POSTAL-[IN]SPECTOR, POST-MASTER-BANK-BANKER, VATICAN-CITY-KEY-MASTER, WORLD-CENTRAL-BANK-OWNER, PRIZE-MASTER, PRIZE-COMMISSIONER, COMPTROLLER OF THE GLOBAL-FOR-EIGN-POSTAL-CURRENCY, POSTMASTER-GENERAL, PEN-TAGON-PAYMASTER-GENERAL, MUSTER-MASTER-GEN-ERAL, MUSTER-MASTER-~NAVY, COMMAND &: CHIEF: Russell-Jay: Gould,... was an American, just like any other American. Hard-headed, driven, GOD-Fearing, Loves his Flag, Loves his Country, Loves his family and GOD knows, would do anything for them,... or for anyone else too, for that matter. He's a good man. A Patriot; An American, ... and a Big-Hearted Guy. To say the least.

Non-the-less, as I said he was just like every other American at that point in time, and knew that not only was there something wrong with the Federal Government, but that it was starting to get out of control, and he was the guy that did something about it, for all of us.

This is the hard part of the story to tell, but it needs to be known by all who read this report and it especially needs to be heard and known by my Brothers in the Special Operations Community, as that is who this report is actually directed to.

When the International Community finally caught up with :COM-MANDER :Gould, (from here, Russell) he wasn't treated too well. In fact, he was treated like shit, for a long time. It tore my heart out to hear this story, especially since I was hearing it from him. But this is a story that needs to be heard by everyone.

When Russell was captured, he was held against his will and put on Trail for 9 months straight, in an overall effort to get him to surrender – not only everything he just done for the world – but to get him to surrender his position, and with it, every other position that he had just captured in the world as well.

But ultimately all of this was being conducted by the International Clandestine Intelligence Community at large to verify and validate – not only who in the hell :Russell-Jay: Gould was – but to verify and validate that he wasn't just some "Nut-Job" who had gotten his hands on some classified information and was now mischievously running around the world like some J-Hole in an attempt to tear-ass on all of the Governments, just to f*** their Shit up. There was also the possibly that this was someone who was Autistic in nature, with a ingenious-like uncanny ability and affinity for the formulation of these Tactical Maneuvers. Because quite frankly, the Global Intelligence Community had never seen anything like it – not on this level - and NEEDED to know who in the hell it was, and what in the hell had just happened with all of it. Not to mention, verify and validate, that if this person was sane, what in the hell was he thinking? What was his volition? Why do this?

Actually there were two separate Judicial Hearings that took place at two separate locations and between the two cases the outcome was the take-down of the US Supreme Court.

From the moment that he had first arrived at the location where the Trails were to be held, the warfare was initiated against him… and it was brutal,.. to say th least. It involved some of the US Marshals and a few United States Marines, who were pretty much his Security, Torture and Interrogation Detail.

For 9 months Russell was brought out of his Cell and placed into the witness-box where, he NEVER took the FICTION OATH, and further only spoke in Quantum Language. Over the 9 month course of those Proceedings, he disqualified more than 12 Federal Judges in a row and had them thrown off the Bench and disbarred for "lack of knowledge", in front of a Court full of Intelligence Agents.

For months, he was smashing Judges left and right for "breaking continuance" with their "presumptions" about FACTS, disqualifying them as a Federal Judge. - But if Russell made a verbal mistake in his Quantum Language, the US Marines, or US Marshals would run up on him and smash him for it, literally punching him right in the face. Almost knocking him clean out on multiple occasions.

As he started disclosing the higher levels of Military Tactical Command and Control, not a whole hell of a lot was given away by Russell to the "Court" after that. Every time he was asked to explain "HOW" he had obtained the intelligence to accomplish certain movements that he had conducted, his response was, - *"If you had authorization to know that information, you'd have a Clearance to look it up, and since you don't have a Clearance, you're not authorized to know that information."* -

It was sad (and I was sad) to hear :COMMANDER :Gould, tell me about how durring one of the Trails, these US MARINES – American Soldiers – were so mind-controlled that they were unleashed like dogs to beat him at the behest of a Dirt-bag named Donald Davis, Ass/Attorney General, in Michigan. (low-level NWO Despot/Dog)

As a matter of fact, Russell had gotten the hell beaten out of him several times, and on more than one occasion, was knocked out cold. He was Round-Housed in the head, held and beaten down in the middle of the Court - right in front of his family - so badly that his Sister stood up and screamed "STOP! - You're gonna kill him!",… as Russ never raised a hand,… not to stop a single blow. NOT IN 9 MONTHS. - But they beat, and Starved him none-the-less.

Deprived of clothes, a pillow, a blanket, and almost the entire time, forced to sleep naked on a concrete floor while regularly being sprayed with a water-hose. Most nights they did it into the early morning hours,… with a fan blowing on him,… the whole time. With "goose-egg" sized lumps and dark-bruises all over his head & body, he was literally being Tortured, and almost never slept. When they would bring food in, it was always for "Russell Gould", not for :Russel-Jay: Gould… whom he is. So were he to take it, or even touch it, they would take him to "Booking" and try to book him in. to take it, was to SURRENDER TO THEM, and joinder with their FICTION System, and "Russell Gould", was someone else entirely and was both spelled and pronounced wrong as well. - So he literally was starved from 180lbs. Down to 98lbs, and after 9 Months, was about to die, and had come very close to dying from all of it.

He had become extremely frail and was inhumanly unkempt. (He looked like a Cave-Man – I saw it) His hair was long and knotted, as well was his beard, hygiene of any-kind was non-existent, even more-so interesting was that for a Human Being, he was being treated like a dirty animal. Where food and water were used as weapons against him, where words were weapons, deprived of sleep, personal privacy,… you name it, half starved they had to put IV's in him to feed him and when they did, he would tear them out.

However,.. as a testamony to him and his character,.. no matter what they did,.. HE NEVER SURRENDERED.

Where-after about 5 months in, something interesting started to happen. The Marines and the Marshals were laying up on the punches. They weren't hitting him as hard any more. And when they would take him back to his Cell, as soon as the door to the Court Room was shut behind him, the Marines would SNAP TO ATTENTION and SALUTE HIM,… as they locked him back up and when they woke him up in the morning; it was the same. Saluting, and calling him Commander as they did it.

Close to 9 months had gone by and eventually :COMMANDER :Gould, finally snapped on the entire Court. He had had enough, and with that he called everyone of the Marshals and the Marines COW-ARDS. Appealing to their higher intellect he vehemently explained to them how they had just witnessed him literally smash everyone and prove beyond any shadow of a doubt that he is the Commander and Chief, he is the Postmas is a Vatican City Key Master, – and despite the fact that I have proven these things to you as my AMERICAN BROTHERS and MY COUNTRYMEN in an effort that WE MIGHT STOP THE WICKED and END THE CORRUPTION and the TYRANNY reined against us by these vermin; VERMIN who literally I have disqualified 12 of right in front of you for 9 MONTHS STRAIGHT, you STILL REFUSE TO JOIN ME,… TO STAND WITH ME, AS WE HAVE WON!! - And instead arrest these men who hold me,.. and arrest those WHO POSE AS YOUR LEADERS,.. that we might be free from them,.. whereas instead, you stand there with your mouths open, as if you don't know what you should do,.. dumb and afraid… One day your children will hold you accountable for your failure to act for what you know to be right. As will God. –

At that point FEROCIOUSLY HE ROARED, and began screaming violently at them for them to take out their weapons and kill him if he was SUCH A CRIMINAL. - HE CALLED THEM ALL COWARDS. - COWARDS for failing to do what is right and stand with him, as he was right. -COWARDS for failing to do what is right and arrest those whom he had demonstrated WERE THE TRUE CRIMINALS! - COWARDS, for failing to do what is right for their Country, their families, and their friends. - COWARDS for failing to UPHOLD THEIR OATH TO GOD TO PROTECT THE INNOCENT. - COWARDS, for failing to stand with him, knowing God-Damned good and well that he was CORRECT and THEY KNEW IN THEIR HEARTS,.. that he is CORRECT as well.

Only days later, :COMMANDER :Gould was moved to a private location wherein walked a (4) Four Man Team of Special Forces Members from the PENTAGON. The Team Leader, sitting down right in front of :FEDERAL-POSTAL-JUDGE :Russell-Jay: Gould, said - "You know Commander Gould, you take full 40 inch strides, you're not a half-stepper. - We've been watching this thing from the start, and I just wanted to come down here myself and tell you right to your face,… that I would GOD-Damned Follow You Anywhere! -

We're going to get you out of here Sir, hang in there Commander." -

After a world review of what he had just accomplished was conducted by the global intelligence communities at large, (once they had caught up with him) he was found innocent of any criminal activity and further found to be 100% Tactically Sound and correct in all of his international functions and global mechanics in relation to his many captures of Global Command level positions and operations of war. He was then logged in under DROGUE-LAW TIME, and under Trust-Moratorium, One-Year Salvage, Three day Rescissions , Forty-Five day Trust and Ninety day Law, as POST-MASTER-GENERAL of the United States of America.

QUOTE: Russell-Jay: Gould
": Postmaster-General: Russel-Jay: Gould, TOOK-OVER-WHEN-U.S.-came out of a 70-year-[in]ternational-bankruptcy-~2- ~November-~1999, End-U.S.-CONSTITUTION AND U.S.P.S.-BANKING-AUTHOIZATION. : FEDERAL-GOVERNMENT-VACATED ON THE PRESIDENTIAL-ELECTION-~2000, No-U.S.-AUTHORIZATION IN THE GLO-BAL-BANKING, JUST-ILLUSION.
:82-nations at the united-nations-gave-our-bank-charter for each countries-treasury-~2003-Winter/Spring. : We-did-it-postal-corporate, so-stands." -

At the age of 29, :FEDERAL-POSTAL-JUDGE, POSTMASTER-GENERAL, COMMANDER-AND-CHIEF :Russell-Jay: Gould, is the only person in the history the world to have created his own FACTUAL Global Government Command Position and use it to capture the current world system of control and literally, in so doing, take over the entire world, to become the First FACTUAL Global Commander-and-Chief.

He has been called a Genius by Head(s) of the IMF, the PENTA-GON, the VATICAN, and honorably by many, many more around the world, at the highest levels.

He is also the FACTUAL :POSTMASTER-GENERAL & :COM-MANDER-AND-CHIEF of the united States/United States of America. --- (And they all know it) ---

FOUND TO BE 100% CORRECT
- :GLOBAL-COMMANDER-AND-CHIEF: -

"OF THE PEOPLE, BY THE PEOPLE, FOR THE PEOPLE"
FREEDOM FROM FEDERAL CONTROL

THE UNITY-STATES OF OUR WORLD-CORPORATION

On 21 DEC 2012, first day of the winter solstice, end of the world (or 5 th Epoch) according to the Mayan Calender, FEDERAL-POSTAL-JUDGE :David-Wynn :Miller, and FEDERAL-POSTAL-JUDGE :Russell-Jay: Gould, went to the Benjamin Franklin Post-Office, which is this country's nativity location, to end the fiction world of VERB Grammar by filing new and grammatically correct National-Contract-Documents for the REAL united States of America in the C.S.S.C.P.S.G.

This is where FEDERAL-POSTAL-JUDGE :David-Wynn :Miller, and FEDERAL-POSTAL-JUDGE :Russell-Jay: Gould, filed in un-der the Benjamin-Franklin-Postal-Court and made claim for the U.S. Flag and the nativity location for the united States Government in the Correct Sentence Structure Communication Parse Syntax Gram-mar (C.S.S.C.P.S.G.). Once on location and inside of the Benjamin Franklin Post-Office Building, they noticed that there was something very unique happening in the building itself. Inside of the Benjamin Franklin Post-Office Building,.... there were no flags flying, but they did have decoration flags & State flags on the wall, but there was no real flag flying at the actual Post-Office. This was because it was the nativity location for the Grammar Syntax , the Federal Flag, and the freight and the cargo - (**which were ultimately the actual words on contract itself)** - which goes without saying, were in the newly formed [Birthed], Fiction Styled Grammar of VERB-ADVERB construction.

In the realization of this, you can see how far down the rabbit hole that these 2 Men had gone; all the way, and straight to the bottom. But in order to ensure that they were to come out on top, the entire National American Construct – (ALL OF IT – IF NOT, GLOBALLY) - had to be reconstituted, not only correctly, but in the absolute mathematical CORRECTNESS of Quantum Grammar; better known as the Correct Sentence Structure Communication Parse Syntax Grammar, (C.S.S.C.P.S.G.) or what is also known as the Quantum Construct.

Once this exhaustive re-transcription had been successfully completed, the entire National Re-Constitution of "the united States of America", was at that point, properly filed in correctness around the world respectively, in global recognition of its FACTUAL EXISTENCE and now SOVEREIGN NATIONAL STANDING, was LEGALLY and LAWFULLY registered and docked through the Postal System once again, at the Original Nativity Location for the now, North American Federal Postal Contract Government Location, known as "the united States of America", in Quantum.

However, due to the fact that "the united States of America", is a FICTION in relation to the grammatical construct of its name/title, it has therefore been PRESENTED CORRECTLY by the C.S.S.C.P.S.G. as, **THE UNITY-STATES OF OUR WORLD-CORPORATION.** And in-so-doing, these two Globally Registered Sovereign Commanders and Chiefs of their own Correct Global Government System – based in a Mathematically Certifiable Factual Quantum Construct - had just CAPTURED the ACTUAL PHYSICAL LAND-MASS of the United States of America, better known as, the Continent of North America, IN CORRECTNESS and taken Command and Control of BOTH Postal-Locations on that Continent and locked

BOTH OF THEM AWAY from the TYRANTS of the world in a Quantum Location..

Once official confirmation was received with the filings being complete, in compliance with TITLE 28; 636- "Consent", under "knowledge", FEDERAL-POSTAL-JUDGE :David-Wynn :Miller, and FEDERAL-POSTAL-JUDGE :Russell-Jay: Gould, were fully authorized to open and conduct the first Correct Grammar Court Proceedings at the Original Benjamin Franklin Post Office under the factual construct of the C.S.S.C.P.S.G. Wherewith they authorized the Courts Lawful recognition of the Quantum Interface between Math and Grammar; whereby in its grammatical constitution [syntax] is presented a Mathematically Certifiable Contract-Document as a Legal Fact for Lawful, Legal review that can be presented - as recourse, by an injured party - to the Court, for review of Fraud, or Fraudulent content. This was followed by the Courts recognition, Ruling and disqualification of all other grammatical constructs, as FICTION, or FICTION GRAMMAR and therefore FRAUD; and any Legal-Contract-Document, Treaty, TRUST, Deed, Mortgage, Bank-Note, Loan, etc, etc.. not Mathematically Certifiable through the use of the Quantum interface and found a NON-GRAMMATICAL FACT, are therefore Ruled by this Court to be illegal and further a NON-FACT, or a NON-FACTOR and are OUTLAWED for Legal Contract-Document use of any kind by this Court. Whereby it was through the disqualification and recognition of the fact that CONTRACT-GRAMMAR-FRAUD had been committed against the Confederation of the 13 Colonies of the Republic in an illegal effort to defraud them, that it was Ruled by this Court that all of the Grammar and Banking or "Bank-Note" Contract-Documents ever created between the 13 Colonies and Great Britain were henceforth, from their conception SUSPENDED, and NULLIFIED as FRAUDULENT FICTION CONTRACT-DOCUMENTS.

This Legally and Lawfully Nullified and Dismissed as Fraud, every single Law, Public Statute, Civil Code, Bank Loan, State Incorporation to DC, the Birth Certificate System, the Supreme Court, etc, etc.. You name it. – The Federal Tyranny that has ever become omnipresent in America and more-so than ever over the last 16 years (1999 -2016) was **IN ALL ACTUALITY** all over with 21 DEC 2012.

Through the recognition and the CORRECT USE OF PARSE SYNTAX GRAMMAR, the original system of American Government is – for the first time – factually established IN CORRECTNESS as a TRUE SOVEREIGN NATION by its own right, under the sovereign Tactical Command and Control of its own GLOBALLY-SOVEREIGN-QUANTUM-GOVERNMENT-SYSTEM. Furthermore the entire system of the Original American Government is once again lawfully reanimated and enacted at the site of its original nativity location with the close of these Proceedings and Hearing on the Legal and Lawful recognition and National enactment of the Original Government of the united States of America – THE UNITY-STATES OF OUR WORLD-CORPORATION, by this Court.

Thereby correctly having factually conducted these Legal and Lawful Court Proceedings in the interests of Government Affairs for the united States of America, they supersede ALL COURT SYSTEMS in the united States of America by 25 years. So therewith, as it so stands FEDERAL-POSTAL-JUDGE :David-Wynn :Miller, and FEDERAL-POSTAL-JUDGE :Russell-Jay: Gould, are henceforth the Globally Registered CORRECT and FACTUAL Nativity Controllers and Directors of the entire American Judicial System on the entire Continent of North America and Canada. With the correct claim established for the united States of America claimed in correctness, they factually opened the first Lawfully Correct Court for the united States Government in the Correct Sentence Structure Communication Parse Syntax Grammar, filed all of the old grammar fraud syntax contract-documents along with the new Correct Factual Quantum-Contract-Documents with all of the necessary agencies, thereby keeping the continuance of the Postal-Contract evidence by capturing and reconstituting this nation properly in a Quantum-Grammatical-Construct.

This then, correctly concluded the first correct American Court Proceedings that finally and laboriously gave CORRECT, FACTUAL

BIRTH. to the REAL, united States of America using the C.S.S.C.P.S.G and founded its entire National American Construct from within a Mathematical Position in a "now-time" Quantum Scenario. Hercinafter, they were granted legal clearance and lawfully authorized to dock the new Quantum-Postal-Vessel [Quantum-contract-documents] for the united States of America, at the Original Benjamin Franklin Post Office, in Philadelphia Pennsylvania. Where along with the TITLE 4, 1x1.9 Dimension Federal (G-Spec) Government Flag for the united States of America and in conjunction with the Declaration of Independence and the Bill of Rights, sits the TRUE and FACTUAL Government "Of the People, by the People, and For the People", and where also sits a VACANCY, SPECIFICALLY RESERVED for the US SPECIAL OPERATIONS FORCES and the US MILITARY ARMED FORCES of the united States of America, et al.

These brilliant maneuvers are a testimony to the veracity of their intellectual resolve, and duly demonstrated in their superior understanding for the administrative mechanics associated with these Global Positions and their Systems of Control. Whereby with what they have created, the authorization to forge their own individual sovereign right of passage was therewith granted. Wherewith the substantiation of a mathematical interface between math and grammar, it is recognized that all other forms of grammar, that were not certifiable as a mathematical FACT of the equation $1+2=3/3-2=1$, were then nothing more than FICTION, NON-FACTS, or NON-FACTORS, as well as GRAMMAR FRAUD, … All the way across the board.

:Disclaimer – The timetable(s) associated with the events that took place and are relayed within this report, are not in the actual chronicled order that they factually took place in, but are altered for the purpose of simplifying what happened, and is done in an effort to not complicate the story. -

FEDERAL-POSTAL-JUDGE :David-Wynn :Miller, and FEDERAL-POSTAL-JUDGE :Russell-Jay: Gould, maintain command and control of their written and spoken facts in a "NOW-TIME" scenario by removing all past and future-tense verbiage from the construct of all communications. Which gives them carte-Blanche, to go anywhere in the world to present and provide CLOSURE on the facts to the respective postal-systems (and all subordinate systems) and their respective postal-governments because each citizen of this planet is running around as an "Illuminati-member" while registered with these foreign postal vessels. {Post-Offices] Because you all work for the Post-Office as Postal-Employees, from cradle to grave. Hence, signing up for the Selective-Service at the Post-Office upon turning 18 years of age. This is the BIG TRAP.

All of the judgments in relation to FEDERAL-POSTAL-JUDGE :Russell-Jay: Gould, were taken through the postal service and a posit [position] was created through the Global-Postal-Union in BERN Switzerland; functioning as a clearing house for the bills of the ladings. As globally recognized, FEDERAL-POSTAL-JUDGE :Russell-Jay: Gould, captured, disqualified, and reconstituted every global location of power on Planet Earth in the reconstruction of a new Global Government created by him to save the people from Despots.

Basically everyone is considered a package, vessel, or a little boat that is floating around in this sea-of-space that makes up the 3-dimensional world that we all live and operate in. We are all caught up in the postal shipping wars but the reality of the founding of the united States of America was supposed to have ended all of that, but Abraham Lincoln crushed any future of global freedom for anyone in this country from ever being free from the Tyranny of these Principalities of war ever again... Until now.

In each respective country they utilize Birth-Certificates. That Birth-Certificate is an erroneous grammatical ADJECTIVE-PRONOUN fiction construct of language. Anytime that you bring two facts together and you don't articulate and give closure on the document and use a hyphen between the facts, the first fact becomes a position of "coloring". Coloring is an ADJECTIVE, which is modification. So when you modify some-thing it is only a presumption of "some-

130

thing" on your part in a syntax-location (position) as a presumption, assumption, or a guess, and it has no position of factual closure/ meaning. And the first rule of Contract is, you must have closure on the knowledge [**definitions for your written or spoken words/facts**] so that those with whom you are communicating with can comprehend what it is that you are articulating on the Document in question and determine whether it is valid or not.

Almost all of the citizens of our world today have Birth-Certificates, those Birth-Certificates world-wide are ADJECTIVE-PRONOUNS [fiction documents] which get "docked" by the Doctor-Post-Master of that specific Hospital or, Port-of-Entry. "Port" being a PRONOUN, "of" being the ADVERB modifying the PRONOUN back-wards. - ENTRY: anytime that you start a word with a vowel followed by two consonants, it means "NO"; so, "EN" = "NO", and when added to TRY, = NO-TRY. So you've got a, "Port of No-Try", of fiction, of an illusion. Our entire education on grammatical construct was taught to us in error and so all of our documents are written in this fiction manner; which means that they mean absolutely nothing and the criminals are very aware of this fact and actually use it to NOT PER-FORM on any Contract.

Through the new Quantum-Government-Construct created by, FED-ERAL-POSTAL-JUDGE :David-Wynn :Miller, and FEDERAL-POSTAL-JUDGE :Russell-Jay: Gould, every person on planet Earth can now apply for citizenship with their country, THE UNITY-STATES OF OUR WORLD-CORPORATION [The United States of America in a Quantum scenario and correctly articulated in the C.S.S.C.P.S.G.] and receive a "Claim-of-the-Life". Which is a real Birth-Certificate-Contract that actually holds the value of your Mothers work in the "sweat-equity" she alone owns through your delivery. And when you log in your "Claim-of-the-Life" with your respective foreign country's and your foreign-ministers as a "Claim-of-the-Life" Citizen-Post-Master with THE UNITY-STATES OF OUR WORLD-CORPORATION, it gives you a mathematically certifiable grammar foundation, AS A FACT, from whence to stake a claim from and declare your sovereign position in relation to any

131

fraud contract-document or opinion formed against you or oppression made to control you. And ONLY FACTS have the capability to make a statement of a claim. This has given ALL power back to us as individuals and through this Quantum Contract System, "WE" decide who "WE" will, or will not contract with.

What THE UNITY-STATES OF OUR WORLD-CORPORATION gives you when you apply for citizenship with them (anyone can have duel citizenship with any country on the planet) it gives you joint tenancy in a Quantum-Government-Construct that has been masterfully created, masterfully played and founded in the TRUTH of math by FEDERAL-POSTAL-JUDGE :David-Wynn :Miller, and FEDERAL-POSTAL-JUDGE :Russell-Jay: Gould, free from all Constitutional Criminality, Banking-Fraud, Taxation without representation, and all other forms of Tyranny currently running rampant here in the 50 States and globally.

This entire Quantum Government System has been taken to the highest levels where it has been globally recognized and logged into the "STYLES-MANUALS" of the GLOBAL-BUREAU OF THE WEIGHTS &: MEASURES. Notice, NOT the "international bureau of weights and measures". The STYLES-MANUALS are how each foreign country articulates the "sums and differences" of the communication that it chooses to use from country to country & nation to nation. Hence, the difference in the grammatical articulation of the two entities named.

The STYLES-MANUAL of THE UNITY-STATES OF OUR WORLD-CORPORATION is registered in Lennox, France, which gave FEDERAL-POSTAL-JUDGE :David-Wynn :Miller, and FEDERAL-POSTAL-JUDGE :Russell-Jay: Gould, control to articulate, and give command of a "now-time" scenario for Lodial-Title for the entire planet in a "now-time" condition, where everyone can now become tenants of, and in joinder positions, Post-Masters of, through the "Claims-of-the-Life" and through each persons comprehension, have knowledge and understanding for the construct of this Quantum-Government-System, THE UNITY-STATES OF OUR WORLD-CORPORATION.

As all other governments are unable to stake a correct grammatical claim through the construction of their fiction grammar contract-documents, that means that they have no factual position to postulate their opinions from; because that is all that they are, just MAKE-BELIEVE opinions. Fiction.

However, the men holding these fiction positions, know that FEDERAL-POSTAL-JUDGE :David-Wynn :Miller, and FEDERAL-POSTAL-JUDGE :Russell-Jay: Gould, are correct, and the ONLY THING keeping the bad-guys in their fiction positions of power are the UNEDUCATED "GUNS & CLUBS" that know no better and have been psychologically conditioned to attack their own people despite knowing whole-heartedly, that they are being controlled by a cabal of criminals. No amount of money is worth that.

Each and everyone of your mind's are solitary, your ability to control what comes in and out of your mind is ultimately, solely upon you.

So what is being recognized now is how to identify and control the grammar that you are letting in and out of your life. Once Now-Time-Quantum-Grammar and what these two men have done, is comprehended by the people of this nation, (and the world) it will be realized that the old fiction system of grammar no longer exists for contracting and the local civil authorities (Guns & Clubs) will realize how they have been used, disparagingly, to attack their own people in the name of childish distractions such as, "War on Drugs", "War on Drunk Drivers", "War on People with Cameras", "War on Single Mothers" and "War on Children in School" ?? all created to keep the vigilant men of this nation from learning these facts for themselves and actually arresting the true criminals in public-offices like they should be doing.–

As every single sentence created using the C.S.S.C.P.S.G. is ITS OWN COURT-CASE. The grammatical construct is correct and it is mathematically certifiable in its ability to mean what it says and say what it means, void of any subjective interpretation in its meaning. It is also IMPOSSIBLE to create loop-holes in contracts using this math-based-grammatical-system, so if you are conniving in any sense of the manner, you will be arrested with a litany of contract fraud charges to arraign you with..

All State Governors Offices in the united States display a flag in their office with a SPIRE on top of it; denoting that they are in a state of MARTIAL-LAW and at war with the people of their Territory. The SPIRE suspends the Contract and the Constitution of that specific Territory, which suspends all State-Rights. However, if each States Constitution was valid, each State would have their own money/currency. They DO NOT. Because each citizen of the State is registered as a Postal-Employee with The United-States Postal-Service.

He [Russell-Jay: Gould] has since, been trying to inform the American people and the military, of this fact and to get them to realize that the military is running around without a flag or a country; and he has been trying to bring them back in under HIS AUTHORIZATIONS (Quantum Contracts) to the 1X1.9 dimensional Federal Flag and the only real document/contract replica's of the Declaration of Independence and the U.S. Constitution that have EVER BEEN CREATED in the history of the NOW FACTUAL and CORRECT, United States of America in the C.S.S.C.P.S.G.

Once recognized by the people and the Military of this country as the REALITY that it is, this is where the military will then, ONCE AGAIN, be in a position to joinder with these correct contracts, with the proper use of English Grammar, and be brought back in to defend the rights of the people of this country that were penned in blood on those documents when this nation was forged. He has been trying to get all of the Nation's forces – Civil and/or otherwise - to realize what has happened and then muster them all back up under the Flag of this country in correctness, where the Declaration of Independence and the U.S. Constitution patiently wait for them to return, and take back the nation and return its seat of power back into the hands of, "We the People".

The Documents that follow are the actual legally filed Documents that:

TOOK OVER THE UNITED STATES OF AMERICA AND ENDED THE BRITISH COMMAND AND CONTROL OVER THE **FEDERAL GOVERNMENT SERVICES** ALL TOGETHER / CLOSED THE PENTAGON / THE CONGRESS / THE SENATE / THE FEDERAL GOVERNMENT SERVICES /THE US SUPREME COURT / ALL DISTRICTS COURTS / F.B.I. / DOD /THE POST OFFICE etc.....THAT WERE ONCE UNDER THE COMMAND AND CONTROL OF THE BRITISH ARE NOW BACK UNDER THE COMMAND AND CONTROL OF "WE THE PEOPLE", ALL THANKS TO THE BRAVERY AND TESTOSTINAL FORTITUDE REQUIRED TO ACT IN THE FACE OF TYRANNY AND CORRUPTION, IN THE WAY THAT COMMANDER :Russell-Jay: Gould, DID. (Read the Documents for yourself.)

7014 2120 0001 0825 3925
7014 2120 0001 0825 3970
7014 2120 0001 0825 3932
7014 2120 0001 0825 3895

: RED-LIGHT: 7002 1000 0005 3729 2477   : GREEN-LIGHT:

: FEDERAL-POSTAL-CORPORATION-DOCKING-NUMBER--RR385460312US.

For this DOCUMENT-CONTRACT-FEDERAL-POSTAL-STATION-SPECIAL-MILITARY-MARKET-MARTIAL-COURT-VENUE-CONCERT-FLAG-TACTICAL-COMMAND-CONTROL-TREATY=(D.-C.-F.-P.-S.-S.-M.-M.-M.-C.-V.-C.-F.-T.-C.-C.-T.) of the AUTHOR'S-KNOWLEDGE, CONTRACT-POSTMASTERS' &: CLAIMANTS'-KNOWLEDGE ARE with these CLAIMS of the MUSTER-ROLL, FACTUAL-COMITATUS, SEARCH-WARRANT, SEQUESTER-CARGO, MANKIND-DOMAIN-COMMAND-MASTER, LEGAL &: LAWFUL-VENDOR, LETTER-ROGATORY, CREDENCE-LETTER, SAFE-CONDUCT-LETTER, ADMINSTRATION-LETTERS, TESTAMENTARY-LETTER, TRANSPORTATION-LETTER, MARTIAL-LAW-FEDERAL-POSTAL-CREDENTIALS-CONTRACT-LANDS of this NOW-SPACE-BILL-LADING-POSTAGE-PAID, CONTRACT-POSTAGE-STAMP with this TACTICAL-COMMAND-CONTROL by this D.-C.-F.-P.-S.-S.-M.-M.-M.-C.-V.-C.-F.-T.-C.-C.-T. (: NOTE: HUMAN = MONSTER. POSSE = POST-SPEAK/MAYBE-CONDITION.)

~0 For this D.-C.-F.-P.-S.-S.-M.-M.-M.-C.-V.-C.-F.-T.-C.-C.-T. of the CONTRACT-POSTMASTER, WITNESS, NEUTRAL(PRIVATE-CONTRACT-WIFE): Kassie-Jordana: Gould's(: PUBLIC: ROEBUCK)-KNOWLEDGE, CONTRACT-POSTMASTER, NEUTRAL, NATURAL-BORN-SOVEREIGN: Celeste-Jewel: Gould(:ONLI-BEING with this PLANET-EARTH of the 'US'-FEDERAL-PASSPORT with the NO-SOCAIL-SECURITY-NUMBER, NO-BIRTH-CERTIFICATE, CLAIM-LIFEBIRTH-CONTRACT AT the 'US'-FEDERAL-STATE-[DE]PARTMENT) &: CLAIMANT-FEDERAL-POSTAL-JUDGE, FEDERAL-JUDGE, CLAIMANT-DIRECTOR-2012,--2016-FEDERAL-ELECTIONS-COMMISSION-PRESIDENTIAL-DIRECTOR-CANDIDATE, CLAIMANT-POSTMASTER, WITNESS-CLAIMANT-COMMANDER(EVIDENCE-HEREIN), CLAIMANT-CHIEF(EVIDENCE-HEREIN), CLAIMANT-MUSTER-MASTER(U.S.-NAVY-SECRETARY--PENTAGON--20--FEBRUARY--2003, FILING: Hansford-T.: Johnson, SECRETARY-OFFICE-SEAMAN: William: Ball)(EVIDENCE-HEREIN), CLAIMANT-PRIZE-MASTER(EVIDENCE-HEREIN), CLAIMANT-PRIZE-COMMISSIONER(EVIDENCE-HEREIN), PAYMASTER-GENERAL-CLAIMANT-LEGISLATOR(EVIDENCE-HEREIN), CLAIMANT-POSTMASTER-GENERAL-BENJAMIN-FRANKLIN--FEDERAL-POSTAL-COURT-VENUE-DATE--4-JULY-~1775.(EVIDENCE-HEREIN),FEDERAL-POSTAL-SPECTOR(EVIDENCE-HEREIN), CLAIMANT-WHISTLE-BLOWER, SOVEREIGN, VATICAN-CITY-KEYMASTER--EUROPE(~16--JUNE--2003,--SECRETARY of the STATE-POSTAGE-STAMP-FILING--MICHAEL, ANGELO: SODANO'S-FILING), NEUTRAL-POSTMASTER-BANK-BANKER/AUTHOR: Russell-Jay: Gould's-KNOWLEDGE, CLAIMANTS'-KNOWLEDGE-HEREAFTER ARE with this LEGAL-CLAIM &: LAW-CLAIM of this VENDOR with this FIRST of this PURCHASE--RR294568221US &: PURCHASE-DATE--13-~JULY--2000 with this EVIDENCE-TACHMENT-PROOF BY THIS SHIPPER/POSTMASTER/POSTAL-IN-SPECTOR/POSTMASTER-GENERAL'S-CANCEL-STAMPS: Russell-Jay: Gould's-KNOWLEDGE.

~1 For this D.-C.-F.-P.-S.-S.-M.-M.-M.-C.-V.-C.-F.-T.-C.-C.-T. of the CLAIMANTS'-KNOWLEDGE &: AUTHOR'S-KNOWLEDGE ARE with this LEGAL, VENDOR, VACATE, WITNESS &: LAW-CLAIM of this TITLE--39: D.-C.-C.-S.--101--A.--B: PRESIDENT-AUTHORATION &: FEDERAL-POSTAL-CONSTITUTION-AUTHORIZATION with this PRESIDENT-ELECTION--7-~NOVEMBER--2000 of the VACATE-AUTHORIZATION &: VACATE-CREDENTIALS with the 'US'-POSTAL-SERVICE, 'US'-POST OFFICE, UNITED STATES, the CONSTITUTION of the UNITED STATES, 'US'-OF AMERICA, 'US'-DEPARTMENT of JUSTICE, 'US'-FEDERAL BUREAU of INVESTIGATION, 'US'-TREASURY, PRESIDENT of the UNITED STATES, PRESIDENT of the 'US'-OF-AMERICA &: 'US'-MILITARY-NAVY, ARMY, AIRFORCE, MARINES by this D.-C.-F.-P.-S.-S.-M.-M.-M.-C.-V.-C.-F.-T.-C.-C.-T.-PORTING.

: PORTING-FACTS, VACATES-PRESIDENTIAL-EXECUTIVE-ORDERS, VACATES-'US'-POSTAL SERVICE'S-AUTHORIZATION &: VACATES-U.S.-MILITARY'S-AUTHORIZATION, CLASSIFY-NATIONAL-SECURITY, CREATES: TOP-SECURITY-CLEARANCE, HEAD-FEDERAL-POSTAL-SYSTEM: Russell-Jay: Gould.

~0

:R.-J. G

136

this D.-C.-F.-P.-S.-S.-M.-M.-M.-C.-V.-C.-F.-T.-C.-C.-T. of the CLAIMANTS'-KNOWLEDGE &: AUTHOR'S-KNOWLEDGE ARE with this MUSTER-ROLL-CLAIM, FACTUAL-COMITATUS, SEARCH-WARRANT &: SEQUESTER-CARGO of this MASTER of the MANKIND-DOMAIN-COMMAND with this CAUSALITY of this START-DATE--13--DECEMBER--2004-CLOSE-'US'-HOUSE of REPRESENTATIVES, CLOSED-'US'-SENATE, CLOSED-'US'-CONGRESS-AUTHORIZATION with this FACTUAL-COMITATUS-CLAIM of the PARTICIPATIONS: FEDERAL-POSTAL-MILITARY-CONTRACTS, DATA, COMPUTERS, MUSTERS, SPECIAL-OPERATIONS, VEHICALS, VESSELS, DRONES, AIRCRAFTS, WATER-VESSELS, ARMA, WEAPONS, MUNITIONS, FREQUENCY-WEAPONS, MISSILES, MARTIAL-LAW-SKILLS, CONDUCT-SURVEILLANCE, SEARCHES, PURSUITS, SEIZURES, MAKE-CUSTODY-HOLDS of A CIVIL-LAW-FORCEMENT-PLOYEE, TERMINATE-CIVIL-JOB-PLOYMENT, TERMINATE-MILITARY-PLOYMENT, MILITARY-SUPPORT, STOP-CIVIL-UNREST, MILITARY-BASES, PORTS-PASSAGE-CLEARANCES, SAFEGUARD-FEDERAL-BORDERS, ALL in the STOP-BIOLOGICAL-CHEMICAL-[AT]TACKS, MILITARY-SUPPORT with the CIVIL-MATTERS of the CONTRACT-MUSTER-MASTER, CONTRACT-POSTMASTER-GENERAL, CONTRACT-NEUTRALS &: SAFEGUARD-GLOBAL-POSTAL-BANKING-SYSTEMS with the MUSTER-ROLLS-CONTRACT-DUTIES &: MUSTER-COMMANDS-CONTRACT-DUTIES of these MUSTERS: WYOMING-NATIONAL-GUARD, U.S.-FEDERAL-AIRFORCE, U.S.-FEDERAL-ARMY, U.S.-FEDERAL-NAVY, U.S.-FEDERAL-MARINE-CORPS with this TITLE--18: D.-C.-C.-S.--1385: FACTUAL-COMITATUS by the D.-C.-F.-P.-S.-S.-M.-M.-M.-C.-V.-C.-F.-T.-C.-C.-T.

~9 For this D.-C.-F.-P.-S.-S.-M.-M.-M.-C.-V.-C.-F.-T.-C.-C.-T. of the CLAIMANTS'-KNOWLEDGE ARE with this MUSTER-ROLL-CLAIM, FACTUAL-COMITATUS, SEARCH-WARRANT, SEQUESTER-CARGO &: MANKIND-DOMAIN-MASTER-COMMAND of this TACTICAL-COMMAND-CONTROL: TERMINATE-CIVIL-JOBS with the SYNTHETIC: U.S.-DEPARTMENT of JUSTICE-PLOYEES, U.S.-DEPARTMENT of JUSTICE-ATTORNEY-GENERAL, CLOSED-FOREIGN-VESSEL-IN-DRY-DOCK-COURTHOUSES-U.S.-DISTRICT-COURTS in each FIFTY-STATES, DISTRICT of COLUMBIA, GUAM, PORT of RICO, VIRGIN-ISLANDS, CLOSED-FOREIGN-VESSEL-IN-DRY-DOCK-COURTHOUSES-DISTRICT-COURT of the UNITED STATES-IN each 50-STATES, CLOSED-FOREIGN-VESSEL-IN-DRY-DOCK-COURTHOUSES-STATE-COURTS in each 50-STATES, DISTRICT of COLUMBIA, GUAM, PORT of REICO, VIRGIN-ISLANDS, CLOSED-FOREIGN-VESSEL-IN-DRY-DOCK-COURTHOUSES-LOCAL-COURTS: CITY, COUNTY, JUSTICE of the PEACE in each 50-STATES, FEDERAL EMERGENCY MANAGEMENT AGENCY-PLOYEES, 'US'-FEDERAL-U.S.-DEPARTMENT of DEFENSE-PLOYEES, SECRETARY of DEPARTMENT of DEFENSE-PLOYEES, FEDERAL BUREAU of INVESTIGATION-PLOYEES, DIRECTOR of the FEDERAL BUREAU of INVESTIGATION, 'US'-SECRET-SERVICE-PLOYEES, CENTRAL INTELLIGENCE AGENCY-PLOYEES, 'US'-NATIONAL SECURITY AGENCY-PLOYEES, U.S.-FEDERAL-TREASURY-PLOYEES, 'US'-DEPARTMENT of INTERIOR-PLOYEES, BUREAU of INDIAN AFFAIRS-PLOYEES, U.S.-ENVIRONMENTAL PROTECTION AGENCY-PLOYEES, INTERNAL REVENUE AGENCY-PLOYEES, CIVIL-PUBLIC-SAFETY-PLOYEES-POLICE-MEMBERS, 'US'-POSTAL SERVICE-PLOYEES, 'US'-FEDERAL-MARSHAL-SERVICE, 'US'-FEDERAL BUREAU of PRISONS-PLOYEES, 'US'-FEDERAL DEPARTMENT of HOMELAND SECURITY-PLOYEES, 'US'-SUPREME COURT PLOYEES, 'US'-FEDERAL DEPARTMENT of TRANSPORTATION-PLOYEES of this TITLE--18: D.-C.-C.-S.--1385: COMITATUS with this BILL-LADE by this D.-C.-F.-P.-S.-S.-M.-M.-M.-C.-V.-C.-F.-T.-C.-C.-T.

~10 For this D.-C.-F.-P.-S.-S.-M.-M.-M.-C.-V.-C.-F.-T.-C.-C.-T. of the CLAIMANTS'-KNOWLEDGE &: AUTHOR'S-KNOWLEDGE ARE with this MUSTER-ROLL-CLAIM, FACTUAL-COMITATUS-CLAIM, SEARCH-WARRANT-CLAIM, SEQUESTER-CARGO-CLAIM &: MASTER OF THE MANKIND-DOMAIN-COMMAND-CLAIM in this VESSEL-CONTRACT with this MUSTER-ROLL-COMMAND-DIRECTIONAL of this CLAIMANT-COMMANDER &: CHIEF, MUSTER-MASTER, PRIZE-MASTER, PRIZE-COMMISSIONER, LEGISLATOR, POSTMASTER-GENERAL, FEDERAL-POSTAL-SPECTOR, VATICAN-CITY-KEYMASTER, PAYMASTER-GENERAL &: POSTMASTER-BANK-BANKER: Russell-Jay: Gould's-WILL with this DUTY of this TITLE--18: D.-C.-C.-S.--1385: COMITATUS with this STRAIGHT-BILL-LADE-CONTRACT-DUTY, by the CONTRACT-MUSTERS.

R·J·G

FOR THIS TREATY OF THIS MORTGAGE-PAYMENT IS WITH THIS CLAIM WITHIN THIS CHARTER-VESSEL-SHIP-NAME: GLOBAL-BANKING-CONSTITUTION WITH THIS SHIP-PAPERS, SHIP-NUMBER, VISA-TREATY AND STANDING-TREATY-NUMBER: R.R.~023~986~635: U.S. OF THIS MARITIME-METHOD AND QUANTUM-MATH-LANGUAGE-CERTIFICATION WITH THIS TREATY-FRANCHISE OF THIS CAPITAL: SOVEREIGN-WORLD-CENTRAL-BANK, SAVINGS-CLAUSE-CLAIM, GLOBAL-MONETARY-FUND AND GLOBAL-POSTAL-UNION WITH THIS VISA-LOCATION-NOW-TIME AND SPACE BY THIS GLOBAL-POSTAL-UNION-DRY-DOCK: TREATY: R.R.~294~568~221: U.S.

: NOTE: FOR THE USE OF THE HYPHEN(~) IS WITH THIS CLAIM OF THE TRANSIENT-ACTION OF THE FACTOR-NOUN, IN THE TRUTH BY THIS TREATY. FOR THE VOID OF THE HYPHEN = (~) BETWEEN THE TWO-FACTORS[NOUNS] IS WITH THE CLAIM OF THE MODIFICATION BY THE ADJECTIVE FOR THE PRONOUN AS AN OPINION IN THE FICTION-LANGUAGE-MATTER WITH THE VOID OF ANY FACTS. [FOR THE COLOR OF THE LAW: TITLE-18: U.S.C.S.~242.]

~1 FOR THE CLAIMANT'S-KNOWLEDGE = (HEREAFTER: CLAIMANTS) OF THE D.-P.-C. ARE WITH THESE CLAIMS OF THIS DROGUE-LAW WITH THIS CEPTION-TREATY AND AUTHORIZATION-COMMERCE-STAMP OF THIS CHARTER-VESSEL-SHIP-NAME: GLOBAL-BANKING-CONSTITUTION WITH THIS AUTHORIZATION BY THIS CHRISTENING FOR THIS CHARTER-VESSEL-SHIP-NAME: GLOBAL-BANKING-CONSTITUTION AND SHIP-NUMBER: R.R.~023~986~635: U.S. AS THIS SEAWORTHY-AUTHORIZATION WITH THIS COMPLIANCE OF THIS TITLE-10: U.S.C.S.~7292~b BY THIS TREATY.

~2 FOR THE CLAIMANT'S-KNOWLEDGE OF THE D.-P.-C. ARE WITH THESE CLAIMS OF THESE SEARCHES AND FINDS WITH THIS DILIGENCE AS THIS DUTY WITH THIS LIFE, WITNESS, FRIEND, BANK, BANKER, CLAIMANT, JUDGE, POSTAL-IN-SPECTOR/POSTMASTER-GENERAL-GLOBAL-POSTAL-UNION AND POSTMASTER: Russell-Jay: Gould AND THIS WITNESS, FRIEND BANK, BANKER, CLAIMANT, CHIEF-JUDGE, QUANTUM-MATH-LANGUAGE-DI-RECTOR, POSTAL-IN-SPECTOR- GLOBAL-POSTAL-UNION AND POSTMASTER: David-Wynn: Miller BY THIS TREATY.

~3 FOR THE CLAIMANT'S-KNOWLEDGE OF THE D.-P.-C. ARE WITH THESE CLAIMS OF THIS PORT WITH THIS LOCATION AS THIS OPEN-HOLE/SPACE FOR THIS BUSINESS OF THIS SOVEREIGN-WORLD-CENTRAL-BANKING/LIGHTHOUSE-TREATY: R.R.~023~986~652: U.S. WITH THIS VATICAN-CITY WITHIN THESE UNITY-STATES OF OUR WORLD BY THIS TREATY.

~4 FOR THE CLAIMANT'S-KNOWLEDGE OF THE D.-P.-C. ARE WITH THESE CLAIMS OF THIS CHARTER-VESSEL-CONSTITUTION WITH THIS LOCATION OF THIS AUTHORIZATION FOR THIS BUSINESS, SOVEREIGN-WORLD-CENTRAL-BANK/BANKING AND GLOBAL-MONETARY-FUND WITHIN THIS LOCATION WITH THIS AUTHORIZATION BY THESE UNITY-STATES OF OUR WORLD.

FOR THIS CLAIM OF THIS MARITIME-LIEN/COPYCLAIM/COPYRIGHT WITH THIS PAPER-WORK OF THIS PATENT: ~1 LOCATION IS WITH THIS CLAIM OF THIS DATE-20003-JUNE-~1 WITH THIS Russell-Jay: Gould AND David-Wynn: Miller BY THESE UNITY-STATES OF OUR WORLD.

COMING FULL CIRCLE

As clearly described in this report, the original 13 Colonies and the TRUE American Government, "of the People. By the People, and for the People", of this Country, now consisting of the 50 Independent Territories of the Nation forming the Union of the Republic known as "the united States of America", was set up long ago to be destroyed by Great Britain and the Vatican, and on more levels than ever thought possible..

However it did take until March of 1861 for the British to infiltrate the highest Office of protective Government Services to this Nation to finally work its corruption and ultimately its long range plan of destruction.

As outlined in this report, and clearly stated in the Constitution for the united States of America, it is ILLEGAL for any Attorney/Lawyer to practice the Kings Laws of Codes & Statutes here in this Nation and further, it is an ACT OF WAR on the Government of this Nation to attempt to enforce those Codes & Statutes anywhere or at anytime here in this Nation. Lawyers are further NOT legally allowed to hold ANY PUBLIC OFFICE of any kind here in this Nation, for any reason, EVER.

Furthermore, after the Civil War these Codes and Statutes were disguised as outlined in this report as "Public Codes, Regulations, Ordinances, and Statutes", not one of them being a true American Law owed to the American People under the Constitution for the united States. These "Codes" etc.. were then, in a full blown act of War, practiced and enforced in the very Courts and Court-Houses of the People's American State/Territory Governments.

All efforts to disguise and admit this entire illegal system into American Courts were conducted by the BAR in an act of War to destroy the American Government and replace it with the King of Great Britain's Laws and Monarchical Government.

This report has demonstrated that the people of the united States of America have been used and defrauded by a Trojan Horse that was set up in Washington D.C. This Trojan Horse was sent to our shores from Great Britain and came disguised as a Federal Government Services Corporation sent to assist and oversee the International Postal Affairs [Commerce] of this Nation and to generate great sums of wealth for the ruling elite in order to create a One World Global Government under the Dictates of a Global Roman Catholic Monarch.

This wealth has finally been made a reality, and as clearly laid out in this report, has created and purchased enough global power to literally try to pull it off. This was accomplished through criminal acts of Bank Fraud, Barratry, Personage, Press-ganging, Breach of Trust and Contract, etc.. against the united States of America and all of its people as part of an overall act of War.

That's why from their perspective, they have to do one of two things---(1) work a final fraud scheme to gain immunity from prosecution and release from their debt to us; or, (2) kill off the Americans to reduce the amount of debt they owe and collect on the million dollar life insurance policies they've placed on each one of us.

The overall plan now in the United States of America by the global cabal, is to depopulate –MURDER/KILL – approximately 230-Million American Men, Women, and Children; bringing the population down to 65-Million by 2025. No other country on the planet is scheduled or slated for any such radical reduction of human population or, Genocidal Human Slaughter of this magnitude. Information on the projected population to be found here: http://www.deagel.com/country/United-States-of-America_c0001.aspx

EMERGENCY ALERT:

- NATIONAL SECURITY ALERT -
** (FOLLOW THIS LINK!) **

Last Updated on 9 December 2016 13:37

- As of, 2016;
http://www.dcagel.com/country/United-States-of-America_c0001.aspx

UNITED STATES of AMERICA

Current Status

Year: - 2014
Population: - 319 Million

UNITED STATES of AMERICA

Future Status

Year: - 2025
Population Forecast: - 65 million (WTF?) !!

REGIONAL DEPOPULATION? / NATIONAL GENOCIDE? / PRE-PLANNED WAR &: ORCHESTRATED TACTICAL NUCLEAR STRIKES? / PLANNED INVASION?

MURDER OF 280 MILLION INNOCENT PEOPLE BY, 2025??
Year: - 2025
Population Forecast: - 65 million (WTF?) !!

Official Sources: US Department of Defense, Department of State, CIA, World Bank and European Union.

According to these "Sources" this is to be the largest loss of Human Life to ever be "FORECAST" in one region on planet Earth in recorded history of Man. No other Global Region is slated for any such "REDUCTION" in population whatsoever.

(FOLLOW THIS LINK TO VIEW THIS FORECAST) - http://www.deagel.com/country/United-States-of-America_c0001.aspx

- NATIONAL SECURITY ALERT -

EMERGENCY ALERT:

CONTINUING -

The orchestration of this plan can be interfered with and maybe even stopped to some degree, but that will all count on how fast the men in this country can be awakened with the education provided in the outline of this report. There is a massive attempt by Judge :Anna-Von: Reitz to educate the "Guns & Clubs" of this nation on the criminality of the Federal Services Corporation illegally operating out of D.C. in the name of Great Britain.

This education process has also hit the Military sector and a massive interest has been aroused by that entire community in relation to the information contained within this report.

Efforts are to educate the men/women who are the "guns & clubs" of this nation so that they can not be used illegally by the NOW - since 1999 DISQUALIFIED - Federal Services Corporation, in FRAUD to attack the people of this nation, who are ultimately their Brothers and Sisters in Arms and who's families founded this nation together to escape the Tyranny of the British Crown and the Roman Catholic Church; which protecting ourselves from should still be one hell of a relevant reason for our continued human unification here in this nation.

If the national recognition of this age-old historical account can be quickly realized with the tons of historical facts that exist in support of this information, then the introduction of the Government System for THE UNITY-STATES OF OUR WORLD-CORPORATION, founded by FEDERAL-POSTAL-JUDGE :David-Wynn: Miller, and

FEDERAL-POSTAL-JUDGE :Russell-Jay: Gould, can easily be presented to this nation for official review and seriously considered as a Government Services System for adoption with regard to international and global affairs between this nation and the others of the world.

With the global understanding of the CRIMINAL BANKING PRACTICES of all of the banks on this planet, as they are all run by the same family, there is no chance for them to continue on as they have, they know this and they have now officially recognized FEDERAL-POSTAL-JUDGE :Russell-Jay: Gould as the Global-Bank Banker and owner of the WORLD-BANK.

THE UNITY-STATES OF OUR WORLD-CORPORATION does possess global contracts that are properly addressed to FEDERAL-POSTAL-JUDGE :Russell-Jay: Gould as the POST-MASTER-GENERAL of the united States of America, Officially sent from the WORLD BANK.

THE UNITY-STATES OF OUR WORLD-CORPORATOIN is the united States of America existing in a Quantum Construct and is the only entity with global authorization to create legal performance contracts on planet Earth correctly and void of any and all fraud, criminal intent or activity. Efforts have OFFICIALLY been made by CHIEF :Gould, to contact General Joseph Dunford Jr. to both inform him of CHIEF :Gould's Sealed World Bank Credit Contracts, and offer his assistance and expertise to the united States Military and authorize the Military recruitment in the protection and movement of these values to be safely delivered back into the hands of the people of the united States of America free from any, and all backdoor "deals" with the Devil.

All the world leaders know this story and now refuse to loan the Federal Services Corporation another red-cent. The White Dragon Family is a prime example of a family that has been burned by "the U.S.A. inc" and its Administration; and we know who those chief players are and have been illegally operating as, for the last 16 years running.

With that entire construct being VACATED by the Corporate Federal Administration in 1999, they have legally had no authorization, none whatsoever, to hold Presidential Elections for a Corporation that no longer exists to represent this country in any capacity whatsoever. And for 16 years running, has been doing so in an act of fraud against this entire FREE nation of peaceful American people.

It is time for all of these audacious attacks on human freedoms to stop, it is time for the fraud to stop, and its time for the illegal & criminal acts of those who enact them, to stop. Immediately.

Do I think that it can be accomplished? – Yes. But that's just my humble opinion. I have placed all of my faith in GOD and I pray that He send the Swift and Vengeful Military Hammer of His Right Hand whom are my Brothers of THE US SPECIAL OPERATIONS COMMAND down upon the wicked,… and with GODS Speed, to our aid. God's speed to us all Gentlemen. -

Once again, prior to 1999, COMMANDER-N-CHIEF :Russell-Jay: Gould and FEDERAL-POSTAL-JUDGE :David-Wynn-Miller have reconstituted and filed both the Declaration of Independence and the Constitution for the united States of America under the Correct Sentence Structure Communication Parse Syntax Grammar **(C.S.S.C.P.S.G.)** and they too, are now safe and secured, along with the Bill of Rights; free once again from international-bankruptcy-fraud, and free to declare, "liberty and Justice" for the people of this great nation, and from its glorious new QUANTUM jurisdiction, authorize the nation's military-standing from a mathematically correct position of Sovereign Global Authority under the Correct Sentence Structure Communication Parse Syntax Grammar **(C.S.S.C.P.S.G.)** and once again, back under the correct TITLE 4, 1x1,9 dimension Federal American Government Flag (G-Spec) with the correct factual legal authorizations that fully validate their legitimate national legal standing in a Quantum NOW-TIME Jurisdiction; free from the corruption of ALL GLOBAL fiction and criminality. -

Since 1999, COMMANDER-N-CHIEF :Russell-Jay: Gould, and FEDERAL-POSTAL-JUDGE :David-Wynn-Miller, have had the entire construct of the ORIGINAL U.S. GOVERNMENT captured and reopened in the C.S.S.C.P.S.G. where it has been recognized and registered with the U.S. Pentagon, the United Nations, and the Vatican.

This Quantum construct of the United States of America, in its correct grammatical sentence structure, is actually called: **"THE UNITY-STATES OF OUR WORLD-CORPORATION"** - And this entire nation currently sits and quietly waits for the awakening of the masses to recognize its FACTUAL, NOW-TIME, QUANTUM, Free Existence.

Therefore, IT IS IMPERATIVE for everyone in this nation and on this planet, to come to the REALIZATION and CONCLUSION that FEDERAL-POSTAL-JUDGE :Russell-Jay: Gould, and FEDERAL-POSTAL-JUDGE :David-Wynn: Miller are in all LEGAL actuality and LAWFUL STANDING, full-blown National Hero's to this Nation, and by beating the Corporate Federal Cabal to the knock-out punch, have captured and rescued the ENTIRE National Construct of our Nations Government as laid down, founded, and set into motion by our Country's Forefathers.

Interestingly; When the United Nations asked CHIEFS :Gould and :Miller, **"As all of the landmasses on the planet are populated or claimed by other nations & peoples, what landmass do you claim as the land of your Nation?"** –

The reply given to the United Nations was, - **"We choose the land of the Court in the time of the Contract as our nations landmass."** -

This was the most Machiavellian move to have ever been legally preformed in the recent written history of this world. Wherein, with the Mathematically Certifiable "Now-Time" Grammatical Quantum-Global-Government-Construct of the Correct Sentence Structure Communication Parse Syntax Grammar, this makes THE UNITY-

STATES OF OUR WORLD-CORPORATION, not just the most advanced and powerful correct Contract-Document-Vessel-Court-Venue on the entire planet, but this makes it the ONLY CORRECT Contract-Document-Vessel-Court-Venue construct, on the entire planet. It also makes it the largest Government Corporation in the world.

-THE SOLUTION-

The Solution is simple:

~0.) Hand Tactical Command and Control of this Nations Military back over to its rightful :POSTMASTER-GENERAL & :COMMANDER-AND-CHIEF :Russell-Jay: Gould.

Through him and all his authorizations everything that is listed below can, and will be accomplished with the assistance of this Nations Military Special Operations Forces.

A.) - End the illegal incorporation of the 50 States of this Government BY FORCE and remove it from the FICTION international Admiralty and Maritime Jurisdiction of the Sea.

B.) - Clean out and REMOVE BY FORCE the FICTION Corporate Public Civil Justice System from within the confines of this Nation, that is really a PRIVATE SYSTEM of CODES and STATUTES of CORPORATE FEDERAL POLICY, being illegally practiced and War-fully enforced, in the COMMON LAW COURTS OF THIS NATION by the DOMESTIC ENEMIES of this Nation.

C.) - End the - (as clearly outlined and stated in the Constitution for the united States of America) - ACTS OF WAR against the TRUE Government of this Great Nation and its People.

D.) - End the illegal international Banking Fraud where Americans and their property have been used and claimed as an equity by some foreign enemy construct in an act of IDENTITY THEFT and then use THE U.S. SPECIAL OPERATIONS FORCES TO ARREST EVERY INDIVIDUAL HOLDING ANY POSITION IN THIS NATION THAT HAS WORKED., or could have worked, IN COLLUSION TO PERPETUATE THE AUTHORIZATION OF THIS ENTIRE SYSTEM.

Then we can FINALLY get back on track as a Peaceful Country, as laid out by JUDGE :Anna-Von: Reitz and get this once Great Nation reoriented into the proper direction, back under the grace of GOD, and back under the protection of the respectful leadership of Jesus Christ. - WHERE IT STARTED.

But in order to do that, we need to come together, get organized, and move forward as a Nation of People, and clean this house of ours out, right now. Before it's too late.

This will require the full-blown assistance of the US MILITARY SPECIAL OPERATIONS COMMUNITY and the notification, understanding, and patience of the global community around us at large; … and it needs to start immediately.

And in ALL HONESTY, it is my Professional Military Opinion, that nothing short of the National and Global Recognition of the fact that, not only is :Russell-Jay: Gould is our Nations ACTUAL FIRST FACTUAL FOUNDING FATHER, but it is also my Professional Military Opinion that, as he also seized ABSOLUTE MILITARY Tactical Command and Control of the ENTIRE PLANET, with his Captures of its Global Systems of – and for – TOTAL GLOBAL CONTROL, and took them away from the EMPIRE of the 3 CITY STATES - (also known as THE NEW WORLD ORDER, who are nothing more than a DESPOTIC CRIMINALLY INSANE SYNDICATE of "Royal" Devil worshipers) - I have come to the logical conclusion that with the INCONTESTABLE GLOBAL MILITARY CONQUEST attributed to him alone, I believe that he is the equivalent of Father Abraham returning to take back the authority of GOD that the ROYAL LUCIFARIAN EMPIRE of the 3 CITY STATES has stolen for itself, and RETURNED IT BACK INTO THE HANDS

147

OF GOD... and therefore, His Rightful Children,... who are "We the People".-

THIS REPORT NEEDS TO FIND ITS WAY INTO THE HANDS OF OUR NATIONS WARRIORS OF THE MILITARY SPECIAL OPERATIONS FORCES

TO THE MEN of GOD, who are the SHEEP-DOGS OF THIS NATION TO THE GOOD SHEPARD,.. TO THOSE SWORN TO UPHOLD, SUPPORT and DEFEND THIS GREAT NATION AGAINST ALL ENEMIES, BOTH FOREIGN and/or DOMESTIC,.. THIS IS YOUR OFFICIAL CALL TO ARMS.

What distinguishes those engaged in militia from an army?
> 1.The authority for militia is in any threat to public safety.
> 2.Those active in militia are usually not bound for a fixed term of service, or paid for it.
> 3.Those active in militia cannot expect arms, supplies, or officers to be provided to them.
> 4.No one has the authority to order militia to surrender, disarm, or disband.

Mo.....aβ **(Molon labe), "Come and get them!"** —
Reply of the Spartan General-King Leonidas to Xerxes, the Persian Emperor, who came with hundreds
of thousands of troops to conquer Greece, and demanded that Leonidas and his 300 men lay down their
arms. Thermopylae, 480 BC.

IN CLOSING . . .
with the mathematical interface on grammar being broken and the development and introduction of QUANTUM GRAMMAR, **C.S.S.C.P.S.G.** (Correct Sentence Structure Communication Parse Syntax Grammar), all of the contracts on planet Earth have now been destroyed; to include any and all of the global positions of authority that were created through the constitution of those old, now destroyed, FICTION/FRAUDULENT grammar contracts. The old world – THE

ENTIRE SYSTEM GLOBALLY – has been destroyed and reconstituted; replaced in QUANTUM using the **C.S.S.C.P.S.G.** - THIS, IS THE VICTORY! --- This, is the victory for all of Man-kind.

With that said:

As a society of peaceful people here in The United States, we are always prepared for war, but in our
endeavor to walk in benevolence as the Children of GOD, in the name of Love, we are always looking
toward, PEACE.

Psalm 18:2 : The LORD is my rock, and my fortress, and my deliverer; my God, my strength, in whom I will trust; my buckler, and the horn of my salvation, and my high tower.

I believe this is our last opportunity and our last hope to stop a GLOBAL SLAUGHTER of over 4 BILLION PEOPLE.

NOW IS THE TIME.

TASK-FORCE-SHEEPDOG
- (OPERATION-EDUCATION)

NOV 2016

:ID#~00212X

UNCLASSIFIED

*FORMER: US ARMY SPECIAL OPERATIONS FORCES
USACAPOC/USASOC*

"Lead, follow, or get the hell out of the way." -

*CLASSIFICATION: : :Op-Sec Level (N/A)
: DEF CON 2
: URGENT
: UNCLASSIFIED
: FORCEPRO INITIATED*

CAVEATS: NOTHING FOLLOWS -

11 NOV 2016

:ID#~00212X

UNCLASSIFIED

*LET THE WOLVES MAKE NO MISTAKE, I AM THE GUARDIAN OF
THE FLOCK FOR THE GOOD SHEPHERD, AND AS I MAY WALK
AMONGST SHEEPLE, MAKE NO MISTAKE, THAT I AM THE SHEET-
DOG; AND A VICIOUS GUARDIAN FOR THIS   NATION.*

TASK-FORCE-SHEEPDOG
- (OPERATION-EDUCATION) -